Christianity—not just a Religion

Christianity—not just a Religion

SPIROS ZODHIATES

AMG PUBLISHERS
CHATTANOOGA, TN 37421

Cover Design: Howard Weinstein
Illustrations: Florence Anderson

12-89-2500

Dedicated to
Josephine and Frederick Kronmeyer
Our librarians
who so wholeheartedly give of their time
and whose lives are shining examples of
practical Christianity

Contents

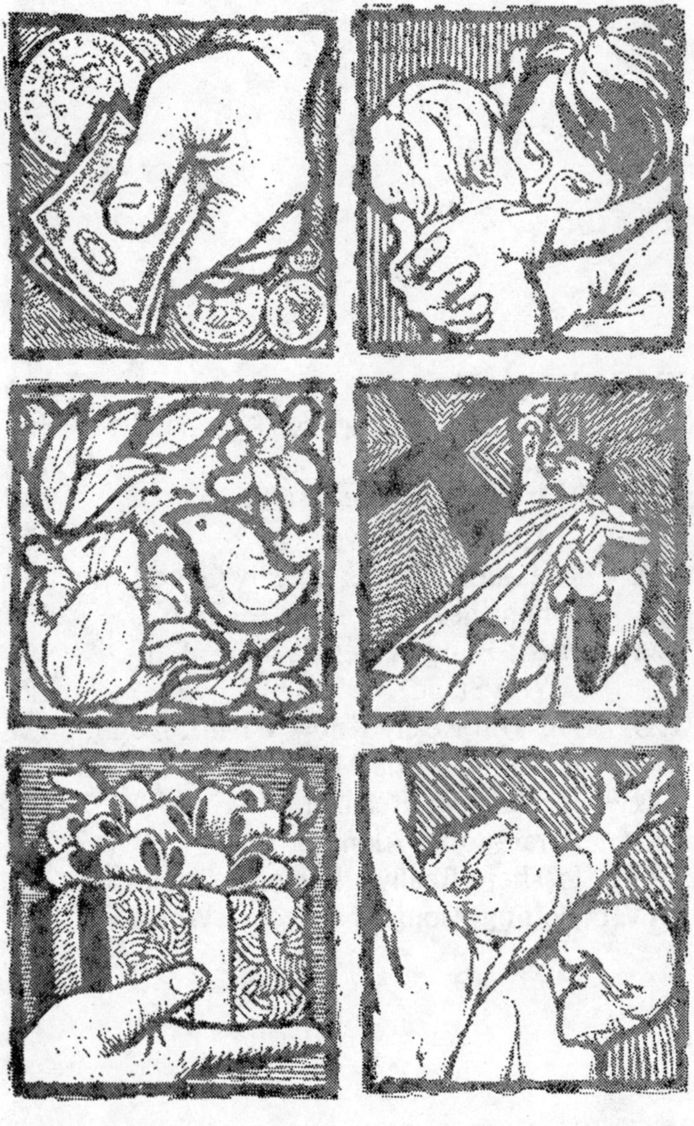

PREFACE

Taxes, death, neighbors, friends, enemies, applause, slander, favors, anxiety, pain, laughter, pleasure, storms, rest—these are some of the things that make up our everyday life. Our attitude toward them shows what kind of Christians we are.

Every week for twenty-eight years I have been writing messages for the Greek newspapers and secular magazines of the world. At random I have picked out a number of these pertaining to "Practical Christianity," and I am presenting them here in English. They have been a test of my own Christian character, and I hope they will prove of practical help to you also in developing and confirming true spiritual values.

To that end I send forth this little volume with a prayer that God will bless it to the reader as He has blessed the writing of these meditations to the author.

—*Spiros Zodhiates*

LAMPS AND SALTSHAKERS

WHAT does it really mean to be a Christian? Are you one? I'm not asking what church or denomination you belong to, but about your own personal experience of Christ. To put it plainly, a Christian is one who has received Christ as his Savior and has made Him Lord of his life. The apostle John says of Christ, *"As many as received him, to them gave he authority to become the sons of God, even to them that believe on his name"* (John 1:12).

If you've done that, not just with the head but with all your heart, then you are commanded to be two things in this world: light and salt. The real Christian, says Christ, is like a city on a mountain; it can't be hid. If you were to visit Athens, it would be impossible for Mount Lykabetos to be hidden from your sight. Its display of light is visible for miles.

You may have some very ornamental lamps in your home, but unless they work they're useless. A lamp's one purpose is to give light. And you don't turn it on in order to hide it under a dark covering. Yet very often that's what Christians—who have been lighted by Christ to shine in the darkness of this world—are doing. They're hiding their light under a bushel, as the Bible puts it. That's why there's so much darkness in this world.

You may also have some pretty saltshakers in your home; but if the salt in them is tasteless, you'd throw it out. The only reason salt exists is to impart saltiness.

The Church today in many places is full of professing Christians who give forth neither light nor saltiness. But if lamps don't give forth light, and salt doesn't give forth saltiness, of what use are they? It would be better to throw them out as rubbish. I'm tempted to say that's where many so-called Christians should go. Christ would lose absolutely nothing. Actually He might gain a great deal, because the world wouldn't have such an unfavorable opinion of Christianity. Ask yourself in all sincerity, "Am I a good advertisement for Jesus Christ in this world?"

People sometimes give as their reason for not attending church that there are too many hypocrites in it. A hypocritical Christian is a contradiction of terms. He belongs neither to the world nor to Christ. An artist sought to portray this sort of hypocrisy. From a distance his picture seemed to be that of a saint in a priestly robe, his hands folded in prayer as he read an open book. However, on closer scrutiny, he was revealed as a dissembler, hiding a large bottle of strong drink. He was a drunkard posing as a saint. Of what use are such saltless, lightless ones to the cause of Christ? They only bring Christianity into disrepute.

What shall we do about the Church when it ceases to preach the pure Gospel of salvation in Christ? At one time there was a flourishing Christian church in North Africa. Where is it today? Its light ceased to be light-giving, and its salt had lost its savor, and it disappeared. Neither salt nor light exist for their own sake, but for the sake of others. Salt gives flavor to food, and light dissipates the darkness. Do you, as a Christian, do this in the life of others? If not, you are useless. Does your church have a good influence on the surrounding community as well as upon its own members? Let's be careful lest our own church suffer the fate of the church in North Africa.

Another artist was asked to paint a church in decline. He didn't picture an old dilapidated building; instead he painted a great cathedral. The interior was beautiful in every detail except one. Near the door, fastened on an ornamental column, was an offering box with a sign over it: "For missions." And over the top lay an undisturbed cobweb. This is a realistic picture of the decaying church. It has nothing to give to those who lie in darkness.

The world around is looking for salt and light. Many are aware that their lives are tasteless, drab, in utter darkness. To you and me as

Christians Christ says, *"Let your light so shine before men, that they may see your good works, and glorify your Father which is in heaven"* (Matthew 5:16). If we do that, they'll see it; they can't miss it.

But let's be careful whom they see. Will they simply see you and me, or the Christ who enables us to be the light of this dark world? Some of us do good works only to show off, whether we acknowledge it or not. If people don't pat us on the back for what we do, we become resentful and unwilling to continue. That shows that the motivation of our service was not divine but human. Works can only be judged as good or evil by their motivation. Christ's works were for the glory of God and the salvation of the sinful and needy.

Remember, Christ didn't say that we were to let our light shine so that men might *hear* about our good works, but that they might *see* them, and thus glorify God. Words are cheap. They can never serve as a substitute for the works of faith. Christ chose physical symbols—salt and light—to show what a Christian should be and do. An orphan, for instance, needs more than words; he needs clothing, food, something tangible to persuade him that there is a God who loves him, and that this God dwells in the hearts of Christians who say they are the light of the world.

Christianity must be practical. Two children were afraid they would be late for school. One said, "Let's kneel down and pray to God that He may help us not to be late." The other child offered a more practical solution: “No, let’s run and pray at the same time.”

Do your part and God will do His. Never expect God to do what you are supposed to do for yourself and for others. But just remember, you can do nothing for the glory of God, if Christ, the Light of the world, has not first entered your sin-darkened soul and saved you. There are works of darkness that try to create light on their own. And there are works of light that are the result of the light of the indwelling Christ. What kind are your works?

THE MYSTERIOUS EFFICACY OF PRAYER

NOBODY likes to fail in any undertaking. It's humiliating and frustrating. But to handle failure constructively we must look for the underlying cause. That's the scientific method. Scientists experiment, fail many times, and try again and again. But the dedicated scientist never gives up hope.

Yet failure can be a salutary experience. It shows up our weaknesses and spurs us on to do better. If we succeeded in everything we undertook, we might become insufferably conceited. Only God is omnipotent. For a human being to become so infallible as to approach omnipotence, he'd have to be absolutely holy and good also, or he'd be a dangerous person indeed. That's why God reserves omnipotence to Himself.

In everything that happens to us in life, we must distinguish the hand of God as distinct from the hand of man. When we are ill, we seek help from a doctor; but neither we nor the doctor must ever forget that ultimate healing rests with God, and is not a purely human achievement. The same doctor may treat two patients with the same disease, one of whom recovers and the other does not. It is God who determines who shall live and who shall die. Man is not the final arbiter of life and death.

Just what place does prayer hold in all this? Christ's disciples performed various miracles in His name. One day, however, they failed to heal a demon-possessed child. When they sought Christ to ask the reason for their failure, He told them, *"This kind goeth not out but by prayer and fasting"* (Matthew 17:21, Mark 9:29). Some critical texts of the New Testament suggest that the phrase *"and fasting"* was added to the text later by a copyist. Evidently he couldn't understand how through prayer alone such humanly impossible healings could be brought about. He felt they needed the human discipline of privation through fasting, as well as prayer. However, Christ placed the greatest emphasis on prayer. He repeatedly stressed what great things could be achieved through it.

For some people, prayer is as natural as breathing. They pray freely and often, speaking as children to their Heavenly Father. Others resort to prayer only when they have come to the end of their rope. They pray only in times of trouble and danger. Be honest. In which category are you?

Then there are the doubters and rationalists.

They hold that everything is ordered by inevitable and inexorable physical laws, and that therefore prayer is unnecessary and achieves nothing. If they believe in God at all, they argue that since He is good and merciful it is unnecessary to ask Him to show goodness and mercy, as if these constituted an exception to His character. "Why should God need our prayers in order to move Him to action, to show goodness and have mercy on us?" they ask.

But Christ told us that prayer does move God to action. How? This is a mystery we cannot comprehend; nevertheless it is a proven fact.

Prayer has other benefits, however, in addition to securing answers to our petitions. For one thing it causes us to sense our dependence upon God. Without fully realizing it, we lose out in our conscious dependence upon the God of the universe because of its very dependability. We don't thank God for the rising of the sun, since this follows a regular pattern. Many people would rarely pray if they were never ill or never met with difficulties. In a very special way when we pray we sense the presence of God, and this feeling is evidence of God's activity in us.

Prayer does something else. It leads us to submit to the will and power of God, as we recognize our own inability and weakness. When we really pray, it is as if we lay our fighting gear in surrender at the feet of the Lord. Or to change the simile, we are like a flower that opens before the sun and absorbs its energy.

God chose man to be His instrument in the world because man is the only one of His creatures to whom He imparts His fullness. In one sense, God imposed certain relative restrictions on Himself in creating man. In giving man authority to the extent that he now exercises it in this world, God limited His own intervention in the affairs of men to some extent. God usually works through man, and if man does not work the works of God, they remain undone. God could have peopled the earth simply by one word from His lips, just as He filled the sky with stars. Instead, He chose a way that to a certain degree depends upon man himself. He made the re-creation of man actually dependent upon each succeeding generation. If men do not reproduce, the earth will remain uninhabited. God could have created the earth so that He would not have needed men, but instead He ordained that men should cultivate it and adorn it. God could have delivered His Gospel to angels to preach, but He didn't. He desires human beings to preach the Gospel to their fellow men.

If God is restricting His activity in your life, it is most probably because you have forsaken the privilege of unceasing prayer. He doesn't do what He could do in you and through you if you really prayed. Great men of God are always men of prayer. Pentecost came after ten days of prayer.

Prayer has the mysterious power to change human weakness to divine strength, strength that is capable of persuading men to come to Christ for salvation. Prayer can also act upon God's will.

Let's not be such fatalists that we think God's will is inflexible. God is open in His activity and disposition toward us. He has a particular plan which He develops for each one of us day by day. God is not restricted by any one of His laws, or by foreordination. He has laws and desires of which we are ignorant. Prayer releases these laws of which we do not know.

At the same time, remember this: God is sovereign, and His will is sovereign, with means to accomplish that will that no one can restrict or inhibit. God's will in its eternal purpose in Christ cannot be thwarted by any man. His eternal purposes must be fulfilled. Malachi 3:6 tells us, *"For I am the Lord, I change not; therefore ye sons of Jacob are not consumed."* And in Numbers 23:19 we read, *"God is not a man, that he should lie; neither the son of man, that he should repent: hath he said, and shall he not do it? or hath he spoken, and shall he not make it good?"*

God's will, as we confess every time we repeat the Lord's prayer, is imperfectly done on earth. That is why we are told to pray, *"Thy will be done."* Man has the option, of course, of resisting God's will but he does it to his own destruction. From our viewpoint, God's intervention in answer to prayer is a miracle. But for God it is the performance of His eternal plan, which we as finite creatures do not know in its details.

Thus we can truly say prayer performs miracles. It accomplishes God's will and purpose. God in His wisdom may not always give us our particular request. He refused the prayer of His own Son in the Garden of Gethsemane, when He cried in agony of soul, *"Let this cup pass from me."* But in a larger sense He did answer that prayer, for Jesus added, *"Nevertheless not as I will, but as thou wilt"* (Matt. 26:39). That prayer was answered; the cross was not bypassed. God's purpose in the plan of redemption of man came to pass through the bitter cup of the cross.

If you do not know Christ as your Savior, I pray that the miracle of redemption from sin may also take place in you. The regeneration of a human heart is no smaller miracle than the healing of a demon-possessed child. But you too must pray; for Satan who has enslaved you can only be defeated through prayer. Your repentance and faith are also needed for this to be accomplished.

DEATH AND TAXES

IT'S a flip saying, but true: those are the two things we can count on. But there's this difference: we know on what day the taxes fall due; we can't predict the day of death. We can put money aside to take care of taxes; but what provision can we make in anticipation of death?

If we die before our taxes are paid, they'll not be forgiven. The government will take them out of our estate. And if we die as unrepentant sinners, our sins will not be forgiven after death. We'll have to pay the penalty for them hereafter.

But there's this difference: God has made a way of escape for us. He's already paid the penalty for our sins—yours and mine. All He asks is that you accept what He has done for you in a true spirit of repentance and faith. However, He does ask that, after you have been forgiven, you yourself will forgive those who have wronged you.

When the angel of death knocks at your

door, how many names will flash across your mind of those you've forgiven? How many will you think of whom you have injured and never asked their forgiveness? How many unconfessed and unforsaken sins will be on your conscience in that hour? If you don't wish your death to be a tragic one, you'd better settle those questions here and now.

The basic question you must face is, Have I been forgiven by God, and have I forgiven others? You cannot have the assurance of God's forgiveness unless you yourself have forgiven those who have offended you. If you claim to be a Christian, you prove it by having a forgiving spirit.

The same is true of love. You prove that you have God's love if you show this love to others; you can't have one without the other. God's Word says *"If a man say, I love God, and hateth his brother, he is a liar"* (I John 4:20). If you can't forgive your brother—and by extension anyone else who has wronged you—it is an indication that you yourself have not been forgiven by God.

In order to have a forgiving spirit, you must first of all recognize your own sinfulness in God's sight and ask for His forgiveness. You can't give others what you yourself have not as yet received.

How can you receive God's forgiveness? Through availing yourself of the provision He has made for your pardon—the blood of Christ shed on the cross to atone for your sins. At the Last Supper, Christ spoke of the cup of wine He held as *"my blood of the new testament, which is shed for many for the remission of sins"* (Matt. 26:28). He said this in anticipation of His crucifixion. His blood was shed for all who would believe in Him and receive Him as Savior and Lord. Christ knew that many would reject His offer of redemption; but there is no one so sinful that the blood of Christ cannot avail for him, if he seeks God's forgiveness.

This is a spiritual transaction. But remember, you are both spirit and body. What you are spiritually must manifest itself in your body—through your actions. You can't just have "spiritual" feelings and not manifest them outwardly. A genuine spiritual experience must transform both body and soul. Of course, many people make the opposite mistake, they seek to do good works without having the Spirit of God within them as their motivating power. They try to offer their good works to God as a basis for their salvation. In effect they are saying they don't need Christ's atonement, since their good works make them acceptable to God. Tragically, they only make them acceptable to themselves; for God regards the works of the self-righteous as "filthy rags."

People don't always like to hear that. They find the cross a stumbling-block. They wrinkle their noses in distaste at mention of the blood of Christ. Surely God could have found some other way, they think. Yes, perhaps He could. He might have done it by just a single word. But He chose a way that was visible to man. It was the invisible love of God for man that led to His incarnation as the Son, in the person of Jesus Christ. *"The Word became flesh,"* so that man could see Him and be entirely without excuse for his unbelief.

One thing must be made clear, and that is that it is not an application of the actual physical blood of Christ that saves us. How limited then its efficacy would be. How could so little blood suffice for all humanity? What Christ did on the cross was to show in His body what He did through His spirit. He loved this sinful race and proved it by humbling Himself to become man and offering Himself as a sacrifice on their behalf. Without this, His incarnation would have fallen short of its goal.

The Apostle Peter tells how God's forgiveness can be secured: *"Who by him do believe in God, that raised him up from the dead"* (I Peter 1:21). Though faith is spiritual, it rests on the material sacrifice of Christ, through which we receive forgiveness. And when, through faith in Christ's atoning blood, we receive forgiveness, it is made evident through our physical actions.

That's why, if you've been forgiven, you must forgive with your whole heart, and show it by your actions toward those who have wronged you. The atonement is not something you can accept in theory. When you receive Christ and His sacrifice for your sins, you are forgiven and your life is changed. If your actions, your bodily habits, your manner of speech, do not change for the better, there is no proof that you have received forgiveness or been "born again." That happens when Christ enters your personality and acts not only through your spirit but through your body also.

You must forgive ungrudgingly; not just in words but also in practice. When Christ spoke of the king who forgave a servant who owed him a great debt, Christ meant that the king wrote off the debt and would never ask for payment from the servant. He didn't say, "I'll forgive you, but you'd better pay the money you owe me as soon as possible."

When you come to Christ and confess that you are unable to pay the debt of your sins, and ask for forgiveness on the ground of His atoning sacrifice, He pardons you at once. He doesn't require your death, because He has already died in your place. He doesn't just forgive you in word; He provided for your forgiveness by a physical act, through shedding His blood. Similarly you, too, are required to forgive others—not just verbally, but in a physical way, by your actions. Go to your enemy and say that you forgive him; and then prove it to him by your loving actions thereafter. Then you will know that Christ really does live in you, and that your sins have been forgiven by God.

GOD AND THE INTERNAL REVENUE SERVICE

HAS the IRS ever called you to come in for an accounting of your Income Tax? They want to be sure you've paid every penny the government believes belongs to it for taking care of its citizens.

I don't know of anyone who faces the IRS representatives with joy. In our subconscious mind we classify them as enemies. We have a feeling they're asking for something that doesn't belong to them. "After all," we reason, "the money we've earned is the product of our own hard work. What right has the government to wring every dollar they can from us?" We begin to think of ways and means to avoid paying any more than we possibly can. And thus a battle begins between the individual and the government.

How different God's government is from man's. God doesn't levy taxes on us. Yet He has far greater power, and offers much more to His citizens, than any earthly government. It would be proper for Him to make greater demands. But instead of imposing taxes He simply asks for voluntary offerings. And how do we respond to such a God? By giving Him the leftovers, or nothing at all, far too often.

Just think of God's love for you. You couldn't live a single moment without it. Did you ever thank Him for the breath you draw—or your eyes, or your ears, or for the fact that you can think? It's impossible to measure God's love for you, whether you are aware of it or not. It's He who has given you life, and He who sustains it. You are God's field, on which He bestows His care. It is He who sows it. There is no man in whom some divine seed has not been planted. True, it often dies, but that is because the ground, your heart, is hard and unyielding. Nevertheless, some seed has been sown in everyone; God speaks to everyone in one way or another. He is the owner; you are His field.

God expects one thing from every field He has sown, and that is fruit. How we misunderstand the purpose of the life God has given us, when we consider longevity His greatest gift. Is this the fruit of life that God expects? Not all of us will see old age, you know. Some will die as children, others as the result of illness or accidents. Fruitfulness in life is not measured by years. Did you ever think that the child God took from your home has performed his divinely appointed purpose in your life, by bringing you to your knees so that you could find salvation in Christ?

The time of harvest will come. The field God has planted must produce. God will send His servants to receive the fruit owing to Him. In that day, what will your response be? Judging by what I have seen of human nature, I think most people want to keep everything for themselves. As they behave toward the IRS, so they behave toward the servants of God. But there is a basic difference between government servants and God's servants. The former use force; they order you to pay. They don't merely request that you give a voluntary offering, as God's servants do.

However, you may not appreciate the fact that God doesn't use force. Note what the farmers in one of Christ's parables did. *"And the husbandmen [farmers] took his servants, and beat one, and killed another, and stoned another"* (Matthew 21:35). Jesus told His listeners that that's how they treated the prophets and others whom God sent during the past. The prophet Jeremiah was thrown into prison; so was John the Baptist—all because they would not tone down God's message. The same thing happened to most of the apostles, and to a great many preachers of divine truth up to the present. Even I, the least of God's servants, have had my share of persecution for preaching the Gospel. I am neither suprised nor frightened by such treatment.

God doesn't use force, nor does He order His servants to use force; not because He can't do it, but simply because He doesn't want to. He wants you to turn your heart and soul over to Him voluntarily. He is not a conqueror but a Savior, not a tax-collector but a Redeemer. The parable would have stopped right there if the servants had used force. But because they didn't, it continues even to this day.

God doesn't stop seeking the fruit that belongs to Him simply because you may be an ungrateful and selfish person who mistreats His servants. *"Again, he sent other servants more than the first: and they did unto them likewise"* (Matthew 21:36). No matter how many of God's servants you scorn and reject, He has more to send you. It's impossible for you to exhaust His patience. He considers your personal salvation more important than even the sacrifice of His servants. Every true servant of God considers the salvation of souls more important than the preservation of his own life.

Death was necessary so that you might be saved from your sin. In the parable, Christ said that the owner of the field finally sent his own son, and the wicked farmers killed him too. And that's just what God did. After men had mistreated and killed His prophets, He sent His own Son to this earth. He knew that evil men would kill Him, just as they had killed His servants. But He didn't hesitate to send Him, and the Son didn't hesitate to go.

The religious hierarchy of that day couldn't tolerate the presence of Christ in their midst. He was a rebuke to them. They knew that they either had to change their ways or kill Him. They preferred to do the latter. But how self-destructive their decision turned out to be! It is just as destructive for you to reject the Son of God who came to harvest your field. It is you who will be the loser, not He.

Sinful man was able to kill Christ, but he could not keep Him in the grave. Christ broke the bonds of death and is now waiting as the living God for you to receive Him. How? By believing that He was sent for your redemption, and in simple faith yielding your heart and life to Him.

A university student who had filled his wall with indecent pictures received an unexpected visit from his mother. She never said a word about them, or gave any indication she had noticed them. But before she left she hung a picture of Christ in the middle of the other pictures. When she visited him again, the only picture hanging on the wall was Christ's. He had radically changed her son's heart.

You can do one of two things: either you can be guilty of killing the Son of God by rejecting His salvation, or you can accept Him and the radically new and different life He will begin in you. Do the latter and live.

"THE CHIEF OF SINNERS"

A LEGEND tells of a young man with a blackened character and a sinful past who came to the cell of a monk seeking forgiveness. As he confessed the terrible sins of which he had been guilty, the monk drew back in horror, feeling his holiness was being contaminated. With an air of self-righteousness he said, "You are wasting your time asking for forgiveness. You are a terrible man. In coming to me you have defiled this holy place. May God grant that on the day of judgment I may stand as far away from you as possible!"

At that moment, the story goes, the voice of Christ was heard saying, "That is exactly what will happen. The desire of both of you will be fulfilled. This sinful young man who repented will enter paradise, and the monk will be kept outside."

You who consider yourself moral, good, and religious, yet draw aside your skirts from contamination with sinners, need to examine your own heart more closely. What are the feelings that fill your mind as you see other human beings wallowing in the filth of sin? Do you instinctively turn away for fear of being defiled, or do you want to win them to Christ by your example and testimony? Surely you don't consider yourself holier than Christ Himself; yet He descended from heaven to mingle with sinners and preach repentance to them.

Nothing repelled Christ more than self-righteousness. A doctor can only help someone who recognizes he is sick and goes to him for help. Is it possible that you are spiritually sick and don't even recognize it? Perhaps that accounts for your restless sense of dissatisfaction.

The Gospel of Christ has been compared to light. *"The people which sat in darkness saw great light; and to them which sat in the region and shadow of death light is sprung up"* (Matthew 4:16). Why light? Because light reveals your real condition. When you are in spiritual darkness you may think you are healthy, when in reality you are sick. The Gospel is light that permits you to see yourself reflected in God's mirror.

Take the Apostle Paul as an example. He was religious—a fanatical orthodox Pharisee—before he came to know Christ. Nobody could persuade him that he was a sinner. But the light of Christ shone on the pathway of his life. The first thing he recognized about himself was that he was a very great sinner indeed. And he never lost this sense of sinfulness even as a Christian.

Before Paul was saved, he spoke of his own righteousness. After his salvation, he spoke of his own sinfulness and of Christ's righteousness—a righteousness that was sufficient not only for himself but also for every other sinner. How different his attitude was from that of the monk of our story. As a Chinese Christian said: "My righteousness is like my shadow. No matter how I bow down, it is always under me. It cannot protect me or anyone else. But the righteousness of Christ is like the shadow of a great rock. It can give rest, and protect more than me." And I ask you, whose shadow are you sheltering under, your own or Christ's?

Many years after Paul repented and asked Christ to save him, he wrote an amazing confession to his disciple Timothy: *"Christ Jesus came into the world to save sinners; of whom I am chief"* (I Timothy 1:15). Can you imagine a pillar of the church today writing to someone and saying, "I am the chief of sinners"? Paul didn't say, "I was a sinner," but "I am." How was this possible? Especially when this same apostle wrote to the Corinthians, *"Therefore if any man be in Christ, he is a new creature: old things are passed away; behold, all things are become new"* (II Corinthians 5:17). And in another place he says, *"I am crucified with Christ: nevertheless I live; yet not I, but Christ liveth in me"* (Galatians 2:20).

How are we to reconcile these statements? When we repent of our sins and accept Christ as our Savior, as Saul did, aren't we saved; don't we cease to be sinners? Is Paul speaking paradoxically; is he contradicting himself?

Notice Christ's commandment in Matthew 4:17. He doesn't say "Repent," which in Greek would be *metanoeesate,* referring to a once-and-for-all repentance, but *metanoeite,* which means "Repent continuously," begin and never cease to repent. When you repent in this sense, you will never again walk in darkness. The light of the Gospel will always shine upon your sin and you will ask for daily forgiveness. When you belong to Christ, you become far more conscious of the presence of sin.

The Christian life has its beginning in the new birth from above. It becomes your entrance into the light of the Kingdom of God. From the moment you are born again, you become a new man or woman, acquiring new appetites, new visions and aspirations as you grow in grace. Things you never previously considered wrong you now recognize as sinful. Your new life is a life full of continuing repentance because you are able to distinguish sin clearly in the light of the Gospel.

One thing Paul made clear, however, is that although he spoke of himself as a sinner, he was a redeemed, a saved sinner. *"Christ Jesus came into the world to save sinners; of whom I am chief."* It is as if he were saying, "Christ saved me, and from that moment on He has continued saving me from every onslaught of sin." Christ is not like a man who rescues you from a shipwreck, brings you to safety, and then leaves you. He is with you all your life. He is not only your Savior, He is also your Lord and Sustainer. Don't be afraid you won't be able to hold out after your salvation. The new nature Christ gives you is one that will find less and less joy in the performance of sin, but will know the joy of finding daily forgiveness and renewal through repentance.

After his salvation, Paul never lost the memory of his sinful past. The more he advanced in holiness the more distasteful his past life became to him. When did he confess that he was the chief of sinners? Not at the beginning but at the end of his Christian life. The higher a Christian ascends on the ladder of holiness, the greater becomes the depth of perception with which he views his sinful past. The more perfect he becomes the more imperfect he sees himself to be as compared to Christ. His holiness is proportionate to his estimate of his own deficiencies and of Christ's all-sufficiency.

AN EXCLUSIVE CLUB WHERE ADMISSION IS FREE

SUPPOSE you were the president of a club. A rich man comes and applies to you for membership. However, your club is made up of poor people and those who belong for the most part to the laboring classes. What would you do? Would you be flattered that a rich man wanted to join, and accept him without question? Of course, it would provide a marvelous opportunity to enrich your treasury.

Besides, suppose this man is not only rich but well educated. The members you've had so far have been plain laborers, fishermen. To accept someone who is both rich and well educated would greatly enhance your prestige. Others might follow his example and ask to join. Your club would achieve status.

What did Jesus Christ do in a similar situation? He is not a mere man, remember. If He were like us, He wouldn't miss the opportunity of accepting into His Kingdom the rich and famous—

but He didn't. This is another proof that He was more than man; He was God incarnate. Man, being a sinner, seldom passes up an opportunity to advance his own interests. Most men are basically opportunists. They're not too squeamish if the advancement of their interests means the sacrifice of moral principles.

Unfortunately, because the leaders of some churches are also opportunists, their example leads some men to conclude that Christianity is a religion of opportunism. But don't look at people. Look at Christ. You don't want to lose out by looking at people who have reduced Christianity to such a level.

Read the story in Matthew 19:16-26 of the rich young man who came to Christ. Relate it to life, for the Gospel is supremely relevant to your problems and mine. *"What good thing shall I do, that I may have eternal life?"* asked this young man. He wanted to enter the Kingdom. The Lord looked at him and realized that he was not only rich but also a ruler with political power. He could have been very useful to Christ in dealing with the hierarchy, who were not in favor of Him. It would seem absurd for anyone in Christ's position not to welcome such a person. But the way He dealt with him proved His deity. Do you know why Christ didn't succumb to the lure of riches and political power this man represented? So that you would recognize Him as God, bow the knee before Him, and say, "My Lord and my God! Save me from becoming an opportunist and make me into a genuine Christian." That's true discipleship.

This young man thought of Christ simply as a good teacher. Usually teachers welcome the rich and give them the red carpet treatment. But every act of Christ showed that He was not merely a teacher; He was God. And only when you approach Him as God will He save you from sin and admit you to His Heavenly Kingdom.

Riches and power can blind ordinary men, because of the hope of gain. But Christ is not an opportunist. He is God who sees the poverty of your soul in spite of your wealth and political power. He declares forthrightly that neither riches nor political power can secure you an entrance into His Kingdom, or bring you peace of heart or forgiveness of sins. Christ is not asking you to do Him a favor. It is you who are in need of His grace. And no matter who you are and what you possess, you can never buy His favor. You must come to Him with the humility of a little child, in simple faith, and say, "Christ, have mercy on me."

Another thing you must recognize is that you can't come to God on your own terms. You can't enter the Kingdom of Heaven because of anything you are, or any good works you have done. In seeking to become a member of any club, you recognize there are certain conditions to be met. God has also set certain conditions for your entrance into His Kingdom. The one prerequisite is the new birth. Christ told another ruler of the Jews, *"Verily, verily I say unto thee, Except a man be born again, he cannot see the kingdom of God"* (John 3:3). *"He that believeth on the Son hath everlasting life: and he that believeth not the Son shall not see life; but the wrath of God abideth on him"* (John 3:36).

This is the real difficulty man faces in his search for a way to enter the Kingdom of God. You cannot find admittance either because of your riches or your poverty. The Kingdom of God is not exclusively for the rich or for the poor. It is only for those who believe in Christ and place themselves at His disposal. Riches and poverty are merely conditions of life. They are not life itself. Christ demands your life, your soul, not merely your possessions. If your life is enslaved by mere things, you, too, like the rich young ruler, will depart from Christ's presence sorrowfully.

In that event, don't look upon Christ as the loser; you are. Of course, Christ is grieved when He sees you reject Him and deprive yourself of His wonderful gift of eternal life. He knows that henceforth your life will be "bound in shallows and in miseries," and therefore you are to be pitied. Is that where you are right now?

Christ's disciples were somewhat dismayed by His behavior. Why lose such an influential person? Here is an opportunity for us to be rescued from poverty, and You turn down the first rich man who asks to enter the Kingdom. That's why they asked, *"Who then can be saved?"* If a moral man like this can't enter the kingdom, who can? Can those who are wallowing in the mire of sin?

Observe Christ's answer. It is very revealing. *"How hard it is for them that trust in riches to enter into the kingdom of God"* (Mark 10:24). This man had more love for his riches than he had for God. He trusted in them for the satisfactions of life. This is why he could not be saved. Nor can you, if you trust in anything but the grace of the Lord Jesus, which is offered to you without price if you will only believe. May you be counted among those who come to Christ on His terms. You will be rejoicing for time and eternity if you do.

HOW TO HAVE A HAPPY NEW YEAR

YOU may not be reading this on New Year's Day, but that doesn't matter. It's appropriate for any time of the year. Just remember,

Every day is a new beginning,
Every morn is the world made new;
You who are weary of sorrow and sinning,
Here is a wonderful hope for you—
A hope for me, and a hope for you.

How often have you said to yourself, "If I only had my life to live over again"? It was probably in some moment of disappointment or realization that you'd made a mess of things. Well, just suppose such a new beginning were possible. What would you put first—education, fame, money, better human relationships? Now is a good time to take stock of just what you want most in life.

We've all made mistakes in the past, and

naturally we want to avoid them in the future. Don't let the mistakes and failures of the past discourage you from trying for a better tomorrow. When a musician plays a piece and misses a note, he doesn't cancel his concert and throw away his instrument. He finishes, but with the ardent desire for a new beginning, which would give him the opportunity to correct his mistake.

When you lose hope of doing better, you lose everything that makes life worth living. A great artist was once asked, "What's the best picture you've ever painted?" "The next one," he replied confidently. But another artist was heard to lament, "Too bad I failed," though he was at the very height of his glory. "Why do you say that?" asked a friend of his in astonishment. "Because I've lost any hope of improvement," he said. He was right; the person who has stopped hoping has truly failed. Is that your state of mind right now?

The hopeful person is one who can learn from his mistakes. In South America there is a tribe of Indians that interprets the past and future quite differently from us. We look at the past as being behind us and the future as lying ahead of us. We may laugh at this tribe as being less advanced than we, but they place the past in the future, and the future in the past. Instinctively they are more discerning than we. Look at their logic: what they've experienced and lived through they place before them to teach them. The sufferings of the past become the lessons of the future. We've known this, but often we haven't practiced it. And they look at the future as lying behind them because it is entirely unknown; it's something that follows rather than precedes them.

It's impossible for you to live the past over again, but this doesn't mean that the opportunities of past years were better than those of the years ahead. Don't grieve over what you've lost, but think of what you can gain. Don't regret what you are not, but think of what you can become. The new can outshine the old.

But how can you achieve this confident spirit? A mother once sent her son on an errand to a place he'd never been. He was a little fellow, but he didn't want to show he was afraid. That's human nature. The younger we are, the more we hate to lose face. Humility often comes with age. As this youngster got ready to leave the house, he stopped at the door, turned to his mother, and said, "It's so far, and I don't know the way. I'm not afraid, you know, but could you come along with me for a little bit of the way?" The mother understood how disturbed the little one was. "Of course," she said. "Mother will come with you all the way." The little fellow put his hand in hers and went out in full confidence that everything would be all right.

You can do something similar as you leave the old year and enter the new. Forget your pride and confess that you have need of a companion who is stronger than yourself. You need someone who knows the way; and that someone is Christ. But you can't just take His companionship for granted. Christ will not consent to walk with you in complete disregard of who you are or what your intentions are. Just as two material elements, oil and water, don't mix, so two spiritual elements cannot mix: man's sinfulness and God's holiness.

You say you believe in God, but—say it, confess it; you are a sinner. You want God to walk with you, but you lack the courage to ask Him. Yet the very reason the invisible and unapproachable God became visible and accessible in the person of Christ was so that He could live among men. *"And the Word became flesh, and dwelt among us"* (John 1:14).

However, before Christ with His divine personality, power, and knowledge can become your companion, either you must change or He must go against His character. That He is not willing to do. This is quite evident from the first message of John the Baptist and of Christ Himself. *"John did baptize in the wilderness, and preach the baptism of repentance for the remission of sins"* (Mark 1:4). He wouldn't baptize people without preaching to them first; and what he preached was that they had no right to be baptized unless they first repented. And Christ said, *"Except ye repent, ye shall all likewise perish"* (Luke 13:3). Repentance is your part in seeking reconciliation with God. Forgiveness is God's privilege. If you repent, He will never turn you away. But if you refuse to repent, He warns that you will *"perish"* and be deprived of His fellowship forever.

The greatest blessing that can come to you is

the assurance that God has forgiven your sins. But you say, "What do you think I am, a criminal?" Well, where did you get the idea that criminals are the only ones in need of forgiveness? As a human being, you were born a sinner. God's Word declares, *"For all have sinned, and come short of the glory of God"* (Romans 3:23). You may regard yourself as a moral and upright person, but in God's eyes you need forgiveness just the same as the worst criminal. Don't make the mistake of considering yourself an exception to this rule.

A fourteen-year-old girl who had just accepted Christ was asked what repentance was. Here is her wise answer: "Before I was saved, I tried to please myself and was not at all sorry for my sins. In fact, I didn't consider myself a sinner at all. When I accepted Christ, I wanted to please Him first. If I ever displeased Him, I was extremely sorry. Since I have been born again, my greatest desire is to please Him." Begin the new year, whether in January, July, or any other time, with such a turn of mind, and I promise you that it will be the best year of your life.

THE BEST WAY TO TAKE REVENGE

HAVE you ever been unjustly accused, or slandered? Has anyone ever betrayed your trust, or defrauded you of what was rightfully yours? I'm sure you've undergone one or more of these unhappy and disturbing experiences. They happen to all of us at one time or another. We can't avoid them. All we can do is to control our reactions to them.

Of course, we're not always the innocent parties we'd like others to believe us to be. Some of the things that happen to us are our own fault. It's not only what we do and say that is important, but what we fail to do or say. If we call ourselves Christians, yet fail to help someone in need when it's in our power to do so, we've sinned. And sin is not only speaking evil of another; it's also failing to come to the defense of someone who is unjustly attacked.

A good example of someone who met unjust treatment in the right spirit is Joseph in the Old

Testament. Take time to read his story in all its wealth of detail to appreciate his character. Think of that scene when his brothers stood before him in Egypt and realized that this was their brother, the one they had sold into slavery in order to get rid of him.

Here was a golden opportunity for Joseph to take revenge. His brothers stood before him, hungry, helpless, strangers in a strange land. How tempted a less magnanimous man might have been to give them the punishment they so richly deserved. Here were the very ones who had tried to kill him. But Joseph was a type of Christ. When the hatred of men nailed our Lord to the cross, He cried, *"Father, forgive them; for they know not what they do"* (Luke 23:34). But we know that was not the end. He rose from the dead and became the victor in spite of all human hatred.

Now was Christ's hour of power. But how did He use it? Not for revenge on His enemies, but for their redemption. He rose from the dead, not to take vengeance on sinful men, but to justify all who would repent and turn to Him in faith. That's what the Word of God means when it says that Christ rose for our justification (Romans 4:25).

When Joseph's brothers realized that their despised younger brother had become a powerful ruler in Egypt, second only to Pharaoh, they trembled at what he might do to them. But Joseph said, *"Fear not: for am I in the place of God? But as for you, ye thought evil against me; but God meant it unto good, to bring to pass, as it is this day, to save much people alive"* (Genesis 50:19, 20).

It's only human for men to take revenge, and to be afraid of revenge, for that's the way of the world. The man whose life is not motivated by Christian principles thinks he has a right to "get even." The man who fears God lets God do the work. God is the only One who can be trusted to judge and recompense men justly and righteously. He is omniscient, while our own knowledge is often deficient. This is why we sometimes judge people unjustly. And often the only reason we don't take revenge for real or fancied injuries is our own fear of retaliation.

Would Joseph's brothers have treated him so cruelly if they had known that some day their own lives would be in his power? I doubt it. This would have restrained them. Yet they would still have been sinful because of the hatred in their hearts. The person who is law-abiding because he is afraid of being arrested and imprisoned for the crimes he would like to commit, or because he fears public opinion, is not really a good man. He is a criminal at heart, just as guilty in God's sight as the one who commits the crime. The one who refrains from taking revenge because he is afraid of the consequence of his actions will be judged for his smoldering hatred just as much as if it had broken out in fury on his enemy.

The words of Christ in Luke 6:31 were spoken to His disciples, and by extension to all who profess to follow Him. *"And as ye would that men should do to you, do ye also to them likewise."* If everyone followed that advice, this world would be a paradise. This is what Joseph did when his brothers stood before him in helpless fear. He put himself in their position, realizing that there might come a moment in his life when he would be standing before a higher power, as his brothers were standing before him.

We never know what may happen to us in this world. It's never safe to assume that, because we have no need of anyone at the moment, this will always be the case. Circumstances change. One day we may be in a position of authority, the next in a prison cell, as Joseph was when Potiphar's wife falsely accused him. One day we could be millionaires and the next beggars. It may be tomorrow that we will need the help of someone against whom we'd like to take revenge today. We must let every action toward others be governed by the answer to this question: "If I were to find myself in their place, how would I like to be treated?"

Criminals would like us to set them free so they could resume a life of crime. A liar wants to be free to tell more lies, an adulterer to commit adultery, a destroyer of property or reputations to continue his destruction.

Christ does not teach passiveness and non-punishment. He was not speaking to sinners here, who terrorize and prey upon society. If Christ had taught that we should treat wicked people as they wish to be treated, the result would be chaos. I for one would not want to live in such a society, although unfortunately our society, as it continues to develop in a climate of misunderstanding of what constitutes freedom, is heading in that direction.

Christ was speaking to Christians, to His disciples. When we confront a sinner, we are to do what we would like others to do to us, if we were in his lost condition. We have come to know the freedom that Christ gives to those who place their trust in Him. He liberated us from the bonds of sin. Therefore we want other sinners to find salvation in Him. That's what we would have liked if we were to find ourselves back in our sinful condition. Now that we have become regenerated, we are supposed to do everything possible to bring the sinner to Christ. We are told to love our enemies. Loving them means working for their salvation. It is the only way they will cease to be our enemies. That is the only way a Christian is commanded to react toward those who do them an injury—to return good for evil.

HOW TO REACT TO SLANDER

IN politics a good name often becomes a football in the hands of a rival candidate. He drops it in the mud and kicks it around at his pleasure. It's a sad commentary on unregenerate human nature that a good name can often be defamed, and a bad name often whitewashed for the sake of gain.

But what should the Christian do whose name is dragged in the mud? You'd think everyone would speak well of the person who is seeking to follow Christ. Seeing Christ in him, they should hold him in high esteem. But they didn't do this to Christ when He was on earth, and Christ said they wouldn't do this to His followers. *"Blessed are ye, when men shall hate you . . . and cast out your name as evil, for the Son of man's sake"* (Luke 6:22).

As Christians, those who are truly born-again and seeking to serve our Master, we naturally want to preserve our good names. But if no one ever says anything defamatory about you, it may be that you are compromising with the world just so people will think well of you. In this world, Satan and his followers are out to attack real Christians. That is why Christ sounded a warning when He said, *"Woe unto you, when all men shall speak well of you!"* (Luke 6:26). The key word there is "all." If unregenerate men speak well of you, it may be that you have been pleasing them instead of your Lord. Your aim should not be to court the good opinion of all. The Christian who is outspoken for His Lord will be both loved and hated. This is what happened to Christ, and *"the servant is not above his Lord."* So don't let unjustified criticism get you down. It would be better for you to be disturbed if "all" men were to speak well of you.

How would you react if you saw a libelous statement about you in some publication? If you were not a Christian, you might curse the one who slanders you. If you had sufficient power, you might even shut down that newspaper or magazine. But as a Christian, Christ forbids you to pay others in the same coin they pay you. Instead He says, *"Love your enemies, do good to them which hate you, bless them that curse you, and pray for them which despitefully use you"* (Luke 6:27, 28).

But, you may object, how can I do good to an evil man or woman? How can I love someone who hates me? Don't misunderstand Christ's meaning here. He is not advocating a sentimental attitude toward evil. What He is saying is that all your actions toward those who are abusing you must concentrate upon changing the evil-doers. If you allow them to continue their evil ways, they haven't ceased being your enemies. If they seek imprisonment or any other just punishment to bring them to themselves, or to protect society, then such punishment must be imposed.

But watch your own attitude in all of this. Be careful you are not rejoicing in the fact that your enemy is getting what he deserves. Don't look upon the retribution that falls on him as vindication for you, but as something that will hopefully bring him to repentance and lead to his salvation in Christ. On the other hand, if being merciful and withholding punishment has a better chance of correcting him, then follow this procedure. Your purpose must never be simply the punishment of the one who is abusing you, but his correction, his salvation, his redemption. Is that your attitude toward those who defame you? If not, it may be that you need a little more of the grace of Christ in your life.

Recently I received a letter from a man in Cyprus who had been saved as a result of reading my newspaper sermons there. He was provided with a Bible, which he read through twice in three months. Now this man knew that in his village there was great enmity between many of the families. So he went among them and shared the Gospel of Jesus Christ with them. And a miracle took place! Men became reconciled who had not spoken to each other in twenty years. This is what Christ can do.

Here is some practical advice on this matter:

Don't believe what you hear from the enemies of Christ about other Christians. Don't even believe a Christian who speaks ill of another. Above all, don't repeat unsubstantiated reports. If it concerns something that you must take action about, prove or disprove the accusations by going directly to the persons involved. I asked someone who began to correspond with me if he knew another Christian in his town. He wrote back that the second man was a very wicked person. I refused to believe his unsupported word, and neither should you believe rumors and gossip about your brothers and sisters in Christ.

Those who speak evil of others are usually too quick to draw conclusions. If they see a man coming out of a bar, they immediately decide he must have been drinking. They lack the charitable nature that would let them consider that he might very well have gone in to distribute Christian tracts in a place where they were desperately needed. Or he might have gone in to try to persuade a weaker brother to leave the place and go home.

What did the uncharitable say about Christ? *"The Son of man is come eating and drinking; and ye say, Behold a gluttonous man, and a winebibber, a friend of publicans and sinners!"* (Luke 7:34). And yet Christ was often thirsty and went hungry for our sakes. But if He had lived as an ascetic, depriving Himself of food and drink as a way of life, He would have been accused of being antisocial.

A busybody is often interested in telling only half the truth. It's true that Christ kept company with publicans and sinners, but it was not because He loved and practiced their sin, but so that He could influence and win them.

A defamatory article about a Christian appeared in a newspaper. It was really terrible. "You must sue him," a friend said. "No," was the answer. "I shall try to set him straight. I'm afraid if I sue him I shall do something that is improper. I learned early in life, and from long experience, that man's character can only be harmed by himself. The first step for me to win my detractor is to overcome my own passion for vengeance."

Reputation is what other people think and say of you. But character is what you yourself decide it shall be. And if you belong to Christ, then your decision will be to be like Him—and by His grace you can be.

MIXED MOTIVES

ARE you a churchgoer? If so, why do you go there? To worship God? Perhaps that's one of the reasons, but there may be others. Human motives are usually mixed; some are stronger than others. We go to church not only to meet God, but also to meet our friends and neighbors.

Perhaps someone who reads this is a medical doctor. One of your motives for adopting that profession was to alleviate human suffering, to heal the sick. But you may also have been motivated by the fact that this profession would give you social distinction and financial rewards above the average. Thus you were led to become a physician by mixed motives, and who can honestly assess which was stronger?

This is true also of many other activities in life. Perhaps you have political ambitions. One of your motives may be a desire to serve your community and your country. But isn't there mixed with this the motive of becoming famous and attaining personal distinction?

We see this principle of mixed motives clearly in connection with the resurrection of Lazarus. After the Lord had raised him from the dead, Christ returned to Bethany, to Lazarus' house. And while He was there, the Bible tells us, something very interesting happened: *"Much people of the Jews therefore knew that he was there: and they came not for Jesus' sake only, but that they might see Lazarus also, whom he had raised from the dead"* (John 12:9). Here we have a classic example of mixed motives. They not only wanted to see Christ; they were curious to see Lazarus, whom He had raised from the dead.

People also take a hard look at us as Christians. Their first motive may really be that they want to visit us; but a secondary motive is to find out if Christians are really any better than those who make no profession of religion. Is this man for real? they ask. And if so, what makes the difference? Some may be honestly seeking, others challenging, and still others skeptical. Whatever their motive in coming to us, we had better exemplify Christ, for they will soon spot a phony.

Again, people go to hear a popular preacher, or they read a sermon because they like a writer. It's so human to be attracted by the appearance and characteristics of well-known public figures, rather than by Christ Himself. But God can use even our mixed motives for our good. He is not like us. He doesn't exaggerate our low motives, or put down our high ones. Many people do just that. They sit in judgment on everybody. They seem to delight in imputing unworthy motives to others, and in this respect perhaps they are judging others by themselves. When they see someone working for the Lord they'll say, "Oh, yes, George is a real saint; but he gets paid for what he does, you know." And the inference is that if he weren't paid he'd not be so zealous for the Lord. It may be that the financial compensation for his work had something to do with his decision to engage in it; but it may not have been his main motive by any means. But it's all too human to exaggerate the secondary motives of others. We seem to derive some sort of satisfaction in pointing out the flaws in their character. It seems that that's the only way some people can build themselves up in their own eyes: by tearing others down. Yet in George's case, a little bit of selfishness may be mixed with the over-riding desire to please God and serve others. Why, then, do we concentrate upon the smaller motive to the exclusion of the larger one? It's a mean and contemptible trait.

God weighs our motives much more justly and mercifully. When we come to church because we want to hear some famous preacher, God can speak so strongly that His voice can drown out the human voice, and this way we are blessed by Him, even though we came to hear a human being. Even our faith in Him is mixed with some degree of selfishness. Underlying our desire for a right relationship with Him is a desire to escape from the consequences of our sin and from eternal punishment. But even if our coming to Christ was motivated by fear, God accepts us as though our motive was love for Him; as indeed it will come to be, once we know Him as Savior and Lord. It may be that, when we decide to give our lives to Christian service, we have one eye out upon the salary we shall receive. But if that is not our primary motive, God accepts us and gives us the salvation of precious souls for our hire—which we will consider a far greater reward than any monetary gain.

It may be the only reason you have picked up this book is out of curiosity. "Let's see what this man has to say." You may be reading this message simply to criticize it, to pick flaws in it. I assure you you'll find plenty, for I'm far from perfect. Nevertheless, whatever your motive, God may speak to you through it. I'm sure Lazarus said to those who were gawking at him, "Look at Christ, not me. He's the one who raised me from the dead."

And I say the same thing to you. Don't look at me. At one time I, too, was dead; dead in sin. But Christ raised me to new life in Him; and what He's done for me He can do for you. You, too, are dead if you are still an unrepentant and unforgiven sinner. In reality, all who have not yet accepted the redemptive work of Christ for their salvation are dead in their sins. The only one who can make you alive is Jesus Christ, because He died for your sins on Calvary's cross, and He rose again that you might live through faith in Him.

Whatever your motive in reading this message, Christ wants to save you, to do for you what He did for Lazarus; not merely to raise your body from the grave some day—though that is part of it—but to give you life through spiritual rebirth here and now. Christ didn't tell the curious crowd that He didn't want them because they'd come mainly to see Lazarus. No matter how mixed their motives, He revealed Himself to them; and He wants to reveal Himself to you also.

And when you become like Lazarus in spirit, a once dead but now living person, people will want to see you, too, along with Christ. Like Lazarus, you'll acquire a sort of attractiveness, as of someone out of the ordinary. People will want to come to ask you about your former life and about your present one.

No doubt people came to see Lazarus because they wanted to know what happens after death, and here was a man who should know. Wouldn't you have been eager to learn about life beyond the grave? Even now, you'd go to the ends of the earth if you knew someone had actually risen from the dead and could tell you all about it.

Well, you can know such a person, if you go to Christ in faith and repentance. Because He rose from the dead, He can raise you to newness of life also. That's what has happened to me, and it can happen to you. How black and hopeless is the hell of sin; and how bright and joyful is the life Christ gives. One who has always lived in the dark doesn't know what light is. The person who has never tasted life in Christ doesn't know what it is. Taste it and find out. Enter the kingdom of the living, by faith in the atoning work of Christ. And then, with Christ, you, too, can become a magnet to attract sinners.

CURE FOR ANXIETY

YOU'D never think of cuddling an enemy, would you? Yet most of us constantly cuddle one of our greatest enemies, anxiety.

You may not even know that you're suffering from anxiety. You don't realize that your irritability, insomnia, and headaches or stomachaches stem from this source. It's a spiritual sickness, but it can be detected from its physical symptoms, even as a doctor detects purely physical ailments from their symptoms, and then proceeds to prescribe the remedy. When you are healed, the symptoms disappear.

We all walk the same road in this life, a road on which we encounter daily burdens and responsibilities. Anxiety will cause us to try to squeeze all the cares of the 365 days of the year into one day. Each day of the year is like a letter sent to us from God. But we tend to want to tackle all of the letters at once. We spread them out before us and promptly begin to tear our hair, not knowing where to begin or where to end. This makes us want to give up even before we start. "How can I find time to read 365 letters?" we moan.

But whoever asked us to read them all in one day? Let 364 of them alone, and tackle just one for today. Do the same thing each day, and you will understand and retain and understand them better. I'm speaking to myself, too, for we preachers are also subject to anxiety produced by a sense of urgency to do our utmost for the Lord. But we are not made to live all 365 days in 24 hours.

Try this simple experiment. Collect 365 little sticks, toothpicks, if you wish. Tie them together. Now try to break the bundle with your hands. No matter how strong you are, you'll never be able to do it. Make a smaller bundle, say 30. You'll still find it difficult to break them. But take just one at a time and, no matter how weak you are, you'll be able to break each one. You're exactly the same person who tried to handle all the sticks together, but this time you changed your way of solving the problem, and it became much easier.

Life has many problems; there's not a day goes by without one. But be wise in facing each day. Change your philosophy of life. Don't try to collect all the problems of the month or year to be solved today. Live one day at a time.

You must breathe in order to live. But you can't breathe today for tomorrow, nor this moment for the next one. If you take in more oxygen than you need now, it can kill you. And if you try to carry the burden of today along with all the tomorrows, you'll find that the resultant anxiety can kill you, too. Anxiety is not only a fear of future, but trying to crowd too much into the present. Whether what you undertake is pleasant or unpleasant, you can't live life all at once.

Listen to a great Physician who knows the human frame because He created it. He is wise; His medicine will bring results if you take it. "Do not be anxious about tomorrow" (see Matthew 6:25, 34). It is Christ's way of warning us not to compress our lives into the present moment.

Work for the present and leave your overconcern for the future in the hands of God, who knows all about it. If it were good for you, He would have revealed the future to you even now. But He knows that to know it in advance might either discourage you from living fully here and now, because of dread of what you knew would come; or, if sudden good fortune were to come to you, might make you sit idly by and wait for it. Either way, such knowledge could do you great harm.

However, God does tell you that your actions and decisions of the present will have future consequences. Your present life is only temporary; it will continue throughout eternity—either in eternal joy or eternal sorrow and regret. And the word of hope He holds out to you for a joyous eternity is, *"He that believeth on him [Christ] is not condemned"* (John 3:18). It's a simple matter of taking God at His word. It's as if He were saying,

"Receive Christ as your Savior, trust in Him, and your future is basically assured and known." You will not be judged and condemned as a hell-deserving sinner, but will be accepted for eternity as a child of God. But that is not true of the one who rejects God's offer of salvation in Christ. The second half of John 3:18 says, *"But he that believeth not is condemned already, because he hath not believed in the only begotten Son of God."* So God has revealed the future of the unbeliever also.

Two men were discussing worry, which one was blaming on God because He didn't let us know what was going to happen. As they walked along, they came to a pasture where a cow was gazing dreamily over a stone wall. "Do you know why this cow has her head stretched over the wall?" asked one man. "No," said his friend. "I'll tell you. It's because she's not able to see through the stone wall. Imitate her. Quit banging the wall with your head. You won't break the wall down, but you will break your head. Stand tall, look over, and you'll be able to see farther on." It's the same lesson the Lord taught when He told people to look at the birds of the air and the lilies of the field, and consider who cares for them. They have less cares than we who can think and reason, but God provides for them, and He will for us, too, if we trust Him.

One night when an ambassador and his valet were obliged to sleep in the same room in a hotel, the valet noticed his master tossing and turning in bed. "Sir, what bothers you?" he asked. "Oh, I have so many things on my mind. The burden of my responsibility is hard to bear." "Forgive me, sir, but do you think God has been governing the world up till now?" "Of course." "And do you think He'll manage even after you've left this world?" "Undoubtedly." "Then don't you think it's possible for you to trust Him to do it even during your lifetime?" The ambassador got the point and was soon fast asleep.

That's what you and I need—faith in the God of the past, present, and future. To know the details of your future life could only increase your anxiety. But trust in Christ who is the Lord of the future will give you peace of heart. It's better for you to know Him than to know all He knows. It's possible for you to become a trusting child of God; it's impossible, with all your forsight, to know what God knows. Which would you prefer to be, a father with myriad responsibilities, or a child with faith in a Father who loves you and who will give what is best for you? I am a child of God because I have accepted Christ as my Savior. If you have done the same, then you have the privilege of casting *"all your anxieties on him, for he cares about you"* (I Peter 5:7).

THE LESSON OF PAIN

ALL of us know what pain is, whether it is the minor annoyance of a hangnail or the excruciating agony of some terminal disease. Pope Pius was right when he declared, "In the garden of humanity, ever since it ceased to be known as an earthly paradise, there has matured and will continue to mature one of the bitter roots of original sin, pain."

There are two attitudes men usually take about pain. One class, those who suffer, often seek comfort from God. But others, those who like to philosophize about suffering, usually declare war against God. It's easy for a person to philosophize about a problem he himself has not experienced in depth.

One day when Christ and His disciples met a blind man, His disciples asked a pointed question: *"Master, who did sin, this man, or his parents, that he was born blind?"* And Christ gave them a straightforward and illuminating answer: *"Nei-*

ther hath this man sinned, nor his parents: but that the works of God should be made manifest in him" (John 9:2, 3).

While it is true that sin brings suffering, Christ wanted them to understand that not all suffering is the result of sin.

When suffering and pain come to us, the first thing each of us must do is to examine himself to determine whether they are the result of some personal sin or of some inherited sin. Don't close your eyes to this possibility. But don't be too quick to ascribe all suffering that God permits in your life as the direct result of sin. Suffering, of course, is always the indirect result of sin. There would be no suffering or pain in this world if Adam, the representative head of the human race, had not rebelled against God, and passed this spirit of disobedience on to his posterity.

As a direct result of their disobedience, Adam and Eve experienced pain: Eve through childbirth and Adam through work, for fatigue in itself is a form of pain and suffering. The result of this suffering, however, was good in both cases: to Eve a child was born, and to Adam the fruit of his labor was the food he produced as he cultivated the ground.

The first sin was occasioned by a desire for knowledge that God wanted to keep to Himself. Adam and Eve reaped the consequences of their disobedience—not the knowledge of God they hoped for, but pain and suffering that they had not expected. Neither now, nor ever in this life, can men fathom the real reason for all the pain and suffering in this world. Thus *"the mystery of iniquity doth already work"* (II Thessalonians 2:7). Man suffered, but he did not learn what he hoped to, as a result of disobeying God. He reaped the consequence of his disobedience, but not the goal.

God not only teaches us obedience through His Word but also through the suffering He sends our way. As someone remarked, "When I get sick, what disturbs me most is not the physical pain, for which the doctors can usually find a reason, but my indifference to the things of God when I was well. Sickness brings to memory the days of health, during which I never thanked God."

Our suffering is related directly or indirectly to our freedom. Sin is the choice of our free will. Most human beings would choose to be good if they could. But since goodness comes only from God, and since through deliberate choice or neglect we have severed our relationship with God, our nature tends inevitably toward evil. Therefore we choose and continue to choose sin and its natural consequence, suffering, whether we realize it or not. When it comes to letting us know what He requires of us, God gives it to us without a "by your leave." But when it comes to that which will produce good in our lives, God needs our cooperation.

If God forced us to do good, it would be His achievement imposed on us, and not the result of our choice. Nothing in itself can be said to be good or evil. The cat that captures birds and eats them does not sin, is not evil. Only man can be good or evil. We cannot attribute evil to a poorly functioning watch. It is more correct to say that the watchmaker did not do good work.

However, though we have the power of choice, even that is corrupt. No man can become good until he is reconciled to God. This is a relationship that he has lost and must renew. This is what is meant by justification. Christ died for man's sin, and if man will receive Him as Savior and Lord, he will be forgiven and experience the new birth. It is then not actually man who performs that which is right, but Christ in him. When man receives Christ, he receives a second nature that will turn him from thinking only of earthly things to the consideration of heavenly matters.

The man who has received this new nature looks upon suffering not merely as an unfortunate occurrence but as a divine lesson. And there are many lessons that only suffering can teach us.

For instance, pain can keep us from greater calamities. It is a warning that something is wrong in our bodies. When it persists, it forces us to consult a doctor. May it also lead us to the Doctor of our souls, Jesus Christ. In Him we will find healing from the sin that so easily besets us.

As a result of our sufferings, we may come to agree with David, who said, *"Before I was afflicted I went astray: but now have I kept thy word"* (Psalm 119:67). Pain stops greater evils, as suffering tests and proves us. It is on the field of battle that good soldiers are proved to be brave.

Few of us recognize our moral weaknesses, but suffering often reveals them to us, and Christ can then help us to overcome them.

Plato was right when he said that no one has a right to become a doctor who has always been healthy. Christ suffered, and therefore He can understand our suffering. He did not deserve to suffer, for He was sinless. But God was glorified through His suffering, which was not really for Himself but for us, for our sin.

Pain is often the proof of God's love. *"My son, despise not thou the chastening of the Lord, nor faint when thou art rebuked of him: for whom the Lord loveth he chasteneth"* (Hebrews 12:5, 6). God's desire for us is to know Him and to become spiritually mature. And suffering is part of that discipline by which He perfects His image in us. The silversmith patiently waits for the fire to purify the silver. And how does he know when the goal is reached? When he sees his image reflected on the silver. God wants to see His image reflected in you. Don't complain about the fire. It's for your eternal good. It will cleanse and purify you. But unlike the silver, you have a choice in the matter. If you refuse to let it cleanse you, it will burn you. The end result is up to you. God wills your eternal salvation and purification. Satan wills your destruction. You cast the deciding vote.

WHY GOD PERMITS STORMS IN YOUR LIFE

DID you know that there are some apple trees that go on strike? Instead of using the nourishment they receive from the earth and the air to produce apples, they just produce wood and leaves. They fail to accomplish the purpose for which they were intended. What does a farmer do when his apple trees refuse to bear fruit? He takes an axe and opens a big hole in the trunk of the tree near the ground; and almost always this has the effect of changing the tree from a state of barrenness to one of fruitfulness.

God does something similar in this world which is His field, when He sees that a life is being wasted. He never acts without a purpose, though oftentimes we fail to understand and profit by it. When He sees a life sunk in torpor or indolence, He often sends a storm to stir it up.

The storms we experience are two kinds, however. Some originate with God in order to do us good. Others are of our own creating. Early one morning the doorbell rang at a pastor's home. There stood a young man, half drunk, in despair, at the end of his own rope. If ever there was a life on the way to shipwreck in a storm of his own creating, it was this young man's. His wife, too, had come through a similar experience. Only 20 years old, she had been married twice, with children by both husbands; had suffered indescribable beatings—a storm of her own making. But in the midst of it all she had seen the face of Christ through the ministry of this faithful pastor. She had been saved by the grace of the Lord Jesus, and her life had been radically changed. Now her husband had come before dawn to wake up the preacher and ask for spiritual help. He could no longer live in the storm he had created.

What had made him come to himself? The recent death of a young soldier killed in the line of duty. The whole town was speaking of this fine Christian lad, now dead. The prodigal husband questioned why God would take such a good man, who was a blessing to the world, and leave him, a miserable sinner, behind. The answer, of course, is that the young soldier was ready to meet his God, while the prodigal was not.

This may be the reason He is keeping you alive. The storms God permits are temporary, but the purpose for which He permits them is eternal. And His basic purpose for your life is the salvation of your soul. There is no greater good where you are concerned. And this can take place right now.

Kneel down and ask God to forgive you by the grace of Christ, who shed His blood on the cross to atone for your sins. That is no doubt why He permits the storms through which you are now passing.

But sometimes God permits storms in the lives of those who have already been forgiven and redeemed, and are serving Him faithfully. You remember that after Christ fed the thousands of people on the shore of Galilee by a miracle, He sent His disciples by boat to the opposite side of the lake. In the darkness they were caught in a storm, not as a result of disobedience, but as the result of their direct obedience to the bidding of Christ. It was He who told them to go. Then why the storm? God does this many times; He places you where you will be tested so that He may show you your need of Him. Don't rebel against this method.

Christ wanted to show His disciples that though they were in familiar waters, they could nevertheless be lost without His presence. He wanted to destroy their self-sufficiency. The disciples knew this sea very well. They were fishermen, and it was here they had received His call. It is humiliating for fishermen to be lost in waters where they ply their trade every day. It's humiliating for you to find yourself unable to cope with the storm in your own life. But Christ knows that if you are not made humble, you won't call on Him to help you. Are you experiencing failure where you thought success was assured? God wants to bring you to the end of yourself so that

He can begin His life in you.

One day the great artist, Michelangelo, stood outside a window. Inside he saw a canvas with a few brushes and paints next to it. All that was missing was the hand of the artist. "Oh," cried Michelangelo, "if I could only be inside, what a picture I could paint!" That's exactly what Christ wishes when He stands outside your life. "If only I could get in, what couldn't I accomplish!" Allow Him to get in. Open the door of your heart. Believe on Him. Then He will bring peace to your troubled soul.

The disciples were so disturbed in the midst of the storm that even the presence of Christ upset them. When they saw Him walking on the sea, they cried out in fear, thinking they saw a ghost. Your ship is also being tossed on the waves. But don't be afraid when Christ approaches. Fasten your eyes upon Him. He's no illusion; He's the only One who can save you.

When Peter asked the Lord to bid him come to Him on the water, the Lord said, "Come." Come; that is what Christ is saying to you also. Peter didn't want to walk on the sea just to perform some miraculous feat; he wanted to get close to Christ. Whatever circumstances the Lord permits in your life, His purpose is to bring you close to Himself.

For a number of years our family had supported an orphan girl in Greece. We finally brought her to the United States to live in our home. One day I took her with me to a church, and while there she gave her testimony. Among other things she said: "God permitted me to become an orphan. Evil men killed my father. My mother died of cancer. But God knew what He was doing. As a result of being left an orphan, I entered a Christian orphanage where I found Christ. If I had not become an orphan, I might never have come to know Jesus Christ."

Christ knows how to dry the tears of an orphan by His presence. He can still the storm in your life if in the midst of it you hear His voice saying, "Come." Will you come to Him now?

WHEN GOD SENDS A MONGOLOID CHILD

A PERSON who suffers will take one of two attitudes toward God: he will either glorify Him or vilify Him. For the sufferer has had time to think, and he tries to find a reason for his fate.

Some time ago I received a letter from a paralytic on the Greek island of Evea. This is what she wrote: "I am late in writing to you to thank you for the literature you sent me about Christ. I wanted to read it because in my great suffering I was thinking about committing suicide. But through reading the New Testament you sent me, I derived courage for life, and I have exercised patience. Praise the Lord, I have been rewarded as a result! I am reading the New Testament for the third time, and every time I read it I find something new.

"A friend came to visit me. She, too, is in great suffering. I showed her the New Testament, and she said, 'Won't you give it to me?' My answer was, 'How can I give it to you? This is my salvation!' With tears in her eyes she begged me to write you to send another so I could give it to her. This would be a great act of kindness on your part, because I just cannot part with mine."

Mrs. V— continues: "I never go out, because my legs are paralyzed. But let God be praised; He knows what He does. It may be that, if I were well, I would be a sinner, and God doesn't want a soul to perish. This is why I declare that whatever God does is for our good. I have been saved. Thank you for your help."

What is your reaction to this woman's attitude? Do you agree with her that God knows what He is doing? Of course, you can only judge from a human standpoint. Your knowledge is finite, incomplete. If you knew all that God knows, if you could penetrate eternity, you could then answer this question with certainty. As it is, you are in no position to criticize or to praise Him. But if you know and have experienced Him in your own life in an intimate and loving relationship, you will know that whatever He sends He means for your good.

Does God really permit paralysis and other incapacitating ailments? Yes, indeed. In Exodus 4:11 He said to Moses, *"Who hath made man's mouth? or who maketh the dumb, or deaf, or the seeing, or the blind? have not I the Lord?"* This was in answer to Moses' complaint that he lacked the ability to speak to the children of Israel on God's behalf.

In the second chapter of Mark's Gospel we read that some friends carried a paralytic to Christ, and he made no objection. I wonder if he would have accepted their invitation if he had been out enjoying the pleasures of a cabaret? Let's face it; when men feel no need of God, He sometimes has to send suffering to turn their thoughts to Him. He knows there is something worse than paralysis of the body; it is sickness of the soul. Good health, prosperity, success often keep men away from the source of eternal life, Jesus Christ.

If you think about it, you will realize that suffering and evil in this world have their ultimate source in the free choice of man—in his liberty to choose God's way or his own way in life. Because man chose to disobey God in the dawn of human history, and proclaimed his independence from Him, God has had to let him reap the consequences of his sin. Actually, however, God is the One who decides who shall be sick and when. We govern and control our lives to a certain point; but beyond that we are forced to throw up our hands like a defeated soldier on the battlefield and say, "I surrender." Empty philosophies cannot help. They don't have the answer to the problem of pain.

God permits you and me to experience either health or sickness, prosperity or poverty, good vision or blindness—all because He wants to speak to us through them. He could, of course, coerce our wills so that we would be forced to obey Him and act properly, turning our eyes toward Him, but He does not, even though this is what we really deserve. But when He chastens us, it is because He loves us. He proves this when He uses our suffering to bring us to Christ. How does a Christian react to suffering? Some with a rebellious spirit, and some with a beautiful faith. For years a devoted minister and his wife had prayed for a child. When a child was finally born to them, he was a mongoloid. The sorrowing minister said to a friend, "My wife doesn't know. I don't know how to tell her."

His friend gave him wise advice. "Read Exodus 4:11 and Romans 8:28 to her: *'Who hath made man's mouth? or who maketh the dumb, or deaf, or the seeing, or the blind? have not I the Lord?' . . . 'And we know that all things work together for good to them that love God, to them who are the called according to his purpose.'*"

When he visited his wife in the hospital later, she said, "I can't understand it. I keep asking to see my baby, but they don't bring him. I'm beginning to wonder."

The husband took her hand lovingly, repeated the verses of Scripture, and then said, "God has blessed us with a mongoloid child."

It so happened that the switchboard operator in that hospital was an atheist who believed that Christianity was a farce. "Christians are like all of us," she said. "Let some suffering come along and they'll break up, too."

When the minister's wife lifted the phone to speak to her mother, the operator listened to the conversation. "Mother, God has given us a mongoloid child. We do not know how or why," she said. There was no hysteria, no complaint. The operator was astonished. She told everybody in the hospital. And on the following Sunday, when the father preached from his pulpit, the switchboard operator and 50 doctors and nurses were in his church. All 50 of them responded to the invitation to receive Christ as their Savior. Can you imagine a mongoloid child being used to bring an atheist telephone operator and 50 doctors and nurses to Christ? This is probably a greater achievement for the glory of God than most Christians could ever accomplish in perfect health.

When we see a paralytic, a blind person, or a mongoloid child, we confess that our judgment is imperfect. As children of God we have the assurance that life is something more, something greater, than what appears on the surface. The greatest tragedy in life is not a dumb person—one who cannot speak—but the man who can and should speak about eternal values, but does not. And the greatest victory in life, and the most convincing proof of God's overruling love even in our sorrows, is the testimony of a suffering saint that God's chastening is for our good and His glory.

BODY AND SOUL

It was a wintry night, so the story goes. A wealthy man was sitting by the fire in his exclusive home. He was deep in thought. Perhaps he nodded a bit. However that may be, suddenly he was startled to be confronted by a stranger, and still more surprised at his words. "Sir," this man said, "I've come to give you whatever you wish. I don't care how precious and rare it is; just name it and it's yours."

The rich gentleman decided to humor him by asking for something seemingly impossible. "I'd like you to show me the *New York Times* dated fifteen days from now," he said.

"That's fine," answered the guest. "Here it is," and he produced a copy from behind his back. The rich man glanced at it, and sure enough it bore a date fifteen days in the future. Eagerly he turned to the business section and looked at the stock market quotations. "Hurray, I've got it made!" he shouted. "I know which stocks are going up and which will go down. I'm going to invest all I've got, with my eyes wide open. I'm going to sell all my stocks that are going to lose, and buy the ones that are going to gain. In this way, in two weeks, I'll really be the richest man in the world."

Having finished with the business news, he turned to other sections of the paper. He read of new developments in the political world, new crimes, and then by chance his own name leaped out at him from the paper. It was on the obituary page. There was the announcement that he had died three days before. He put the newspaper down and cried, "What's the use of trying to make more money, if I'm going to be dead before I can enjoy it?"

The Bible tells of a similar situation. Here are some words God addressed to a rich farmer: *"Thou fool, this night thy soul shall be required of thee: then whose shall those things be, which thou hast provided?"* (Luke 12:20). It seems the farmer had been very wise in making provision for storing an over-abundant harvest. But he had been most unwise in not being prepared for the eventuality of death.

You, too, may have made every provision you deemed wise for the future and your old age. But have you given any thought beyond that? After all, you may never live to be really old, but it's certain you'll have to face death. If you've made no provision for that you've been very foolish indeed.

A woman once asked the famous preacher, John Wesley, what he would do if he knew that he would die tomorrow at midnight. "How would you spend the time in between?" Wesley replied, "Exactly as I am spending my time now. I would preach tonight and again three times tomorrow. I would go to help somebody who needs me. I would have my evening family worship, and at ten o'clock I would go to my room as usual; and at midnight I would deliver my spirit to my Heavenly Father so that I could wake up in His glory."

Death would not have altered the course of John Wesley's life. But if this were you, how would you spend the last day of your life? Would you continue as you have always been doing? You need have no fear of death if you are ready to meet it at any time because you are at peace with God as Wesley was.

I am just wondering, if the rich farmer had known he was going to die that night, would he have said to himself, "*What shall I do, because I have no room where to bestow my fruits? . . . This will I do: I will pull down my barns, and build greater; and there will I bestow all my fruits and my goods. And I will say to my soul, Soul, thou hast much goods laid up for many years; take thine ease, eat, drink, and be merry*" (Luke 12:17-19).

This man's basic mistake was that he thought his soul could be satisfied with material things. He confused the material with the spiritual. Each area has its own needs. It was not sinful that this man should have reaped an overabundance of crops. If God didn't wish it, He could have prevented it. But your wheat, your food, your material possessions cannot satisfy the need of your soul. Your spirit needs spiritual food, just as your body needs material food. It is sinful to neglect either one. Both are gifts of God. Unfortunately, most people pay more attention to the body, to material things, than to the spirit.

It may be that you are rich in material things, but be careful that poverty doesn't overtake your soul. For your body you need bread to fill the stomach. For your spirit you need the food that is found in the Word of God. Never forget the words of Christ, *"Man shall not live by bread alone"* (Matthew 4:4). This is what the man in the parable tried to do. He thought himself rich, but in God's sight he was miserably poor. God could say of him as He did of the Laodiceans, *"Thou sayest, I am rich, and increased with goods, and have need of nothing; and knowest not that thou art wretched, and miserable, and poor, and blind, and naked"* (Revelation 3:17).

The salvation of your soul belongs to the area of the spirit. It may be that you consider yourself religious, and yet you have never understood this basic law of the kingdom of God. It may be that you do kind deeds, and give generously to charitable causes, hoping in this way to save your soul and commend yourself to God. You'll never accomplish it. Your soul, your spirit, the immaterial part of your personality, is estranged from God your Creator, who is Spirit. If God were matter, then your material and physical acts could reconcile you to Him. But God is Spirit (John 4:24), and reconciliation to Him is a spiritual transaction.

A Jewish leader once came to Christ seeking something to satisfy his heart. The Lord told him he must be born again (John 3:3). What immediately came to this man's mind? It was his body. He was a religious leader who should have been conversant with spiritual truths, yet he was confused. *"How can a man be born when he is old?"* he asked. *"Can he enter the second time into his mother's womb and be born?"* (John 3:4).

Listen carefully to Christ's reply: *"That which is born of the flesh is flesh; and that which is born of the Spirit is spirit"* (John 3:6). In other words, when you, and I, and every man, were born into the physical world, we had no communication with the world above us. We knew only the world around us. In order for us to begin to live in the context of eternity, we have to come to believe that there is a world above us and not only the material world around us. To do this, we have to believe God's revelation to us in Christ, who was sent to us from above, and thus be born from above. Only then will we begin to live in the fullest sense of the word, and be ready to die at any time, knowing where we are going. Then the future is robbed of its fears; since neither life nor death can separate us from the love and care of God.

HOW GOOD A NEIGHBOR ARE YOU?

How small our world has become in just one generation! Once formidable journeys have become brief hops from one country to another. There are no isolated countries. The whole world is our neighbor.

But do we really consider all people everywhere our neighbors? Not really, not in the Biblical sense. Some people we like; some we don't. Some we love; some we hate. We can't always find it in our hearts to forget the harm some have caused us. We become very concerned about the area in which we live, in preserving the status quo and keeping out elements we regard as undesirable.

Sometimes it seems that the closer we live to one another the more difficult we find it to live with each other. Some of the most destructive wars of history have taken place, not in past eras when men were isolated, but right in our own age, when distances have been practically eliminated.

We co-habit, we co-exist, but we don't really cooperate to make this a better world; we really don't live together. If countries were not restrained by fears for their own safety, it is altogether conceivable that they might not hesitate in a few minutes to destroy those who do not agree with them. Nations and individuals can be highly intolerant of those who hold different ideologies from theirs—whether they be religious, economic, or social.

But don't think that this problem of living as neighbors is a new one. It may have come into sharper focus now, but it has always existed. The Lord Jesus Christ faced it when He was on earth, and the principles He laid down then are applicable to every time, place, and circumstance.

It seems that a religious leader who was also a lawyer got into a discussion with Jesus Christ on the question, *"Who is my neighbour?"* (Luke 10:29). This question was occasioned by a previous one he had asked Christ: *"Master, what shall I do to inherit eternal life?"* (Luke 10:25). Christ mentioned what was commonly accepted: Refer to the Ten Commandments. This lawyer knew perfectly well what God demanded in the Decalogue. He mentioned the Commandments in summary form: *"Thou shalt love the Lord thy God with all thy heart, and with all thy soul, and with all thy strength, and with all thy mind; and thy neighbour as thyself"* (Luke 10:27). Two things are necessary: love for God and love for neighbor. But the lawyer knew that much depended on the meaning of the word neighbor. If it includes someone who has hurt you or who strongly disagrees with you, it is difficult, in fact almost impossible, to love him.

The lawyer was to be commended for his sincerity, if for nothing else. Another person might have said hypocritically, "That's an easy thing to do. Of course I love God and my neighbor. I don't defraud either one or the other." But as a lawyer this man wanted to know the exact meaning of every word. "A neighbor," who is he?

It may be that he wanted to confuse the issue by debate over this question. By presenting the issue as a very problematical one, he could thus excuse himself for his failure really to love his neighbor. Christ made the correct diagnosis of his attitude: *"But he, willing to justify himself, said unto Jesus, And who is my neighbour?"*

Knowing our own failure many times to fulfill our God-appointed duty toward Him, we realize this is an all-too-human weakness. But to try to excuse ourselves for such failure is inexcusable. It's a trick we've learned from that master of deceit, the devil. When God confronts us with a question, instead of answering Him honestly and directly, we bring up another question in order to evade the issue.

I remember that when I was in high school we had a mathematics teacher who loved to talk. If our lesson was difficult and we wanted to avoid tackling it, one of the students would adroitly put a question to the teacher to get him started. Goodbye to the lesson for that day. We often try to treat God in a similar manner, thinking to distract Him from His subject. When He tells us we must repent in order to be saved from sin, we resort to a philosophical argument as to what constitutes sin. Be careful. God is not an easily distracted professor of mathematics. He knows all our tricks.

Christ didn't answer the lawyer with a definition. He told him the story of the Good Samaritan. At the end, instead of saying, "Here is who your neighbor is," He probed the conscience of the lawyer by asking, *"Which now of these three, thinkest thou, was a neighbour unto him that fell among thieves?"* (Luke 10:36). The lawyer found himself neatly cornered, in spite of all his skill in debate. He was caught in a trap of his own making through the answer he was obliged to give: *"He that shewed mercy on him"* (v. 37). Then Christ commanded, *"Go, and do thou likewise."*

The real question here is not, "Who is my neighbor?" The real question for us is the one the lawyer should have asked: "Whose neighbor am I?" We want others to be neighborly to us, but God wants us to become true neighbors to others. We want to occupy center stage, dominated as we are by self-love and self-interest; but God asks us to make others the center of our love and concern. The matter of neighborliness is solved when we stop expecting others to prove their good intentions toward us and instead prove our genuine concern for them. It's not our neighbors—good, bad or indifferent—who constitute our problem, but ourselves. As a comic-strip character once astutely observed, "We have met the enemy, and he is us."

Do others say the neighborhood in which you live is bad? It may be that you are the disrupting influence, and not your neighbor. So often we want others to be what we think they ought to be, but we seldom think of ourselves as not being what we ought to be. What we do outwardly has its origin in what we are inwardly. We have degraded God's image in us. When God first created man, he bore the stamp of the divine nature; but since the fall he bears a devilish one. God created man to live as a neighbor to his Creator. Instead man became His enemy. He avoids God because His presence condemns him.

Is that the real reason you haven't been able to live comfortably with God? Are you avoiding Him? You'll never achieve peace of heart that way. God still wants to live in fellowship with you. He doesn't avoid sinful men, those who are estranged from Him or at enmity with Him. He sent His Son, Jesus Christ, in order to reconcile us to Himself. Only when we as individuals respond to His divine initiative can we become children of God. Then we will begin to consider everyone our neighbor, not for the purpose of taking advantage of them, but of helping them in their need, and especially of helping them to become children of God.

However, God must first of all be enthroned

in your heart through your acceptance of Jesus Christ as your Savior, if you are to be filled with His love toward others. Don't expect others to take the initiative in befriending you, before you can relate to them. Christ asks you to go out of your way to become their friend first, a good friend and a good neighbor.

SPEAK OUT!

ONLY cowards keep silence when they ought to speak up. The consequences can be destructive. We are not supposed to connive at falsehood. Our indifference makes us liars also. When we know someone is lying, and we allow him to continue, we become accomplices in his crime.

Unfortunately, in a world such as ours, we see liars speaking out boldly and daringly, while truthful persons remain silent and fearful. If you were to ask me what is one of the greatest needs of our times, I would answer, "For people to have the courage to speak out in defense of truth, and to act on their convictions." Unfortunately truth suffers and error triumphs because the silent majority allow it to continue.

When God came down to earth in the person of Christ, His divine intervention was for the purpose of making the truth apparent in a world darkened by sin and error. This is what truth does; it intervenes. It does so without asking the consent of those among whom it acts. It knows it wouldn't stand a chance of receiving such consent. Error never welcomes truth; it rather seeks to choke it. It is afraid to have truth raise its voice; it fights it with every weapon at its disposal.

But for truth to prevail it must never remain inactive or passive. It must never take the blows of error with bowed head. The character of truth is its unchangeableness, its eternal nature. It is like love, of which the Apostle Paul says, *"Love never fails"* (I Corinthians 13:8). And truth never gives in to error. It goes to all lengths, makes any sacrifice, in order to redeem the one who is in error. Truth never seeks to destroy the liar but to convert him. In order to do this, it intervenes, not in a democratic but in a theocratic way. It doesn't seek the votes of those who are enslaved by error, but uses its God-given omnipotence to convince them.

Christ was the incarnation of truth. He declared Himself to be the truth in John 14:6. How did He act to prove it? Not with fear but with courage. As truth He dared to speak and act without regard to the consequences to Himself.

Here is an example: One Saturday He went to the synagogue and, without asking permission of the chief rabbi, began to teach. This was the courage of truth. He didn't go merely to listen, to submit Himself to the traditional religion of the day. He came declaring Himself to be the truth that descended from heaven to show His countrymen there was something lacking in their religion. In many cases it had degenerated to a mere formality. Christ was under divine obligation to intervene, since He knew that He was the truth.

Do you possess the truth of Christ and the courage to declare it without even being asked to do so? If not, perhaps the truth you say you possess is not really the truth of Christ after all. I believe that if the truth we preach is Christ's truth, it must manifest itself in the same way as Christ's did. We need not ask permission first in order to witness for Him. We do it because of the necessity that lies in the character of truth. Truth dares lift up her voice and speak even where she is not wanted because she knows her presence is necessary. Do as Christ did. Don't wait to be asked; declare the truth without fear of the consequences. You'll be surprised at the results, once you give voice to the truth with courage.

Truth dares not only to speak up and teach, but also believes in taking action. Truth speaks and acts, not in a spirit of self-assertion or conceit, of course, but for the good of others.

Witness Christ in the synagogue. He stands up and teaches without permission. Among those who listen is a poor woman whose body has been bent over with suffering for eighteen years. Christ singles her out from the others. Omnipotence searches out those whom no one else can help. His interest extends beyond her soul to her aching body. Why? Because He wants those in the synagogue to understand that God is interested in the whole person. He is never indifferent to the physical suffering of anyone. Teaching becomes mere empty words when it is not accompanied by action when that is necessary. If truth is genuine, it cannot remain indifferent to human pain. If your truth leaves you indifferent to the needs of others, it is not the truth of Christ.

Just as Christ spoke without asking permission from anyone, He also acted. He didn't turn to the chief rabbi and ask, "Is it permitted for me to heal this woman on the Sabbath, since I have the power to do so?" No, He interrupts His teaching, stops speaking, in order to show that His words are not those of a mere man, but that He Himself is life and the giver of it. He turns to the woman and says, *"Woman, thou art loosed from thine infirmity."* Then *"He laid his hands on her: and immediately she was made straight, and glorified God"* (Luke 13:12, 13).

The chief rabbi became highly indignant because Christ had performed this miracle on the Sabbath. On that day, worship to God was limited to words, not works. Again, truth dares speak out—this time to the rabbi himself: *"You hypocrite,"* Christ says to him.

Is He saying that to you who profess His truth and yet keep silent? Let Him speak and act through you. He will give you the necessary courage. Being truth, He takes the initiative. Do not hinder Him.

IS IT REALLY BETTER TO GIVE THAN TO RECEIVE?

WHICH makes you happier, to receive a present or to give one? Tell the truth, now. Isn't it a fact that most people would rather get than give?

Not everybody feels that way, of course. In a moment of great rejoicing over some success in a mission hospital in the African jungle, a famous missionary doctor said, "If my friends everywhere could only comprehend the joy of just an hour like this!"

Or take that young man who spent all his holidays, including his vacation, visiting and entertaining little children in the hospital. Instead of using his leisure hours to have a good time with his friends, as most people do, he went to cheer up sick youngsters by playing with them and showing them films. A society was formed in his honor, and at the conference preceding the inauguration dinner he got up and said, "Tomorrow you'll be having a good time in my honor. I'm sorry I won't be here. But don't you feel sorry for me. I think I'll be having a better time than you with the kids in the hospital."

Christ Himself said, *"It is more blessed to give than to receive,"* and He practiced what He preached. But how did some people react to His gifts? One day He healed ten lepers. All accepted the great gift of restored health, but only one returned to thank Him. The other nine were satisfied to receive the gift without the Giver. Many people seek God only when they're in trouble. Once He has met their need, they forget Him.

If you really knew God as your loving Heavenly Father, you'd consider companionship with Him your greatest treasure. I've heard of a father who had to be away from home about seven months. On his return he took his family to a shopping center. Handing some money to his little girl, he said, "Lydia, take this money and buy anything you want." The child's eyes filled with tears as she clung more tightly to his hand. "What's the matter, Honey?" he asked. "I don't want your money, Daddy," she said. "I want you!"

What do you want from God—what He can give you, or God Himself? When you have Him, you have everything, because He is the Creator, Sustainer, and Giver of all things.

Actually you own absolutely nothing you didn't receive from God in the first place. Men in their unregenerate state are moral lepers. God doesn't owe them anything. The danger is that the more He gives them the less gratitude they will feel or express. The more they receive of His material blessings the less they desire Him. Men have forgotten God, not in an arid desert but in a paradise. If He denies them His gifts, they consider Him hardhearted, without compassion. They really put Him in a very difficult position. If He showers abundance on them, they will be tempted to feel no need of Him. Had Christ not healed the ten lepers, it may be that in their need they would have kept coming to Him and profited by His preaching. He would have had all ten of them. But when He healed them all, He was left with only one out of ten.

You may be sure of one thing. Even if you are sick, as long as you keep in contact with God, you are far better off than if you were healthy and estranged from Him. Can you see, then, that it is really a blessing of God that permits the storms of life—your sickness and other difficulties—because otherwise you might forget Him altogether? These things grieve the heart of God, but what can He do? He knows that the greatest blessing for you is not continual sunshine but companionship with Him. Because He considers this so important, He has to achieve it many times by depriving you instead of giving to you.

The history of the world has often been determined by cycles of abundance and privation. When in man's abundance he begins to forget God, He brings about famine. Study the Book of Judges to see how God treated His people. As soon as they entered Canaan and tasted its abundance, they began to forget the God who had liberated them from captivity and given them all this prosperity.

One of the greatest dangers you and I face is that we will cease to depend upon God for everything. The ten lepers no doubt had exhausted every human means for help. Since they could think of nowhere else to go, they finally went to Christ. But once they were healed, and became accepted again in the society of other men, nine of them felt that was all they needed.

When those around us pat us on the back, we tend to forget that there is One above us whose approval is far more important than theirs. If, however, we find ourselves in trouble, and our friends turn away from us, to whom else can we turn? The prodigal son returned to his father only when his fair-weather friends forsook him. Had they stuck by him, perhaps he would never have returned to his father.

It may be that you, too, are passing through troubled times. You wonder why God permits it. His Word tells us that He chastens those He loves. Perhaps you are not as close to Him as you should be. He wants you near Him. He has a gift for you—your salvation and healing for your humanly incurable sin. But don't come to Him just for that. Of course your spiritual health, your salvation, is very precious. The healing of the lepers was also very precious. But even more precious to the tenth leper was the company he later kept with Christ.

You can't possibly imagine the value of unbroken fellowship with God. Nothing in the world can compare with this blessing. Of course, if Christ is to have you as His companion, He first wants to cleanse you. Whatever your spiritual condition, go to Him and never depart from Him.

It was the Apostle Paul who kept for us that wonderful beatitude of Christ not recorded in the Gospels: *"Remember,"* he says, *"the words of the Lord Jesus, how he said, It is more blessed to give than to receive"* (Acts 20:35). To be blessed means to be satisfied. You'll be far happier giving than receiving. What do I mean by that? Simply that, if you've received the grace and salvation of Christ, you can't help wanting to share it. If you keep it just for yourself, you'll never enjoy it as much as when you share it with others. I don't know whether the grateful leper came to Christ just once to say "Thank You," but my feeling is that he probably came many times after that bringing with him another leper for Christ to heal.

If Christ has healed you from the leprosy of sin, the best way you can say "Thank You" to Him is by introducing as many as possible to Him. If you only knew the joy that comes from leading another soul to Christ, you'd thank Him for the privilege. It's one of the greatest gifts He could give you. Try it and see.

ARE ALL RELIGIONS EQUALLY GOOD?

EVERY rational person thinks. And the product of thinking is called "thought." It's one of those intangibles like love that can't be seen, weighed, smelled, or touched—and yet it's there. It can only be evidenced by its outward effects. Watch a person's face when he's reading a book. What he thinks of it may be indicated by a chuckle, a frown, a sudden nod of the head, and a broad smile of satisfaction as he finally lays it down. "I see you think that's a good book," you may say. No, you couldn't see his thought; you could only deduce it from his actions. Thought belongs to the realm of those invisible entities that cannot be subject to absolute proof.

Or take the realm of nature. We accept it because we can apprehend it with all five of our senses. But when we try to discover the laws by which nature works—though we've uncovered much—I suspect that there are many more physical laws that we don't know about than those we do. Our ignorance is still greater than our knowledge.

However, once we have discovered any of the laws that govern the universe, we proclaim them with absolute certainty, and admit of no rival laws and theories. In school we don't find one teacher saying that two and two are four, and another that two and two are five. Once a physical law has been defined and established, we don't hold that any man's contrary claim is equally valid. The truth of physical phenomena render its laws exclusive.

Yet the human mind often refuses to grant that this holds true regarding the laws of the spiritual realm. They prefer to accept the glib assumption that all roads in the religious world lead to God and heaven. The argument goes something like this: "There's only one God, and every religion is based on serving and following and worshiping that one God, by whatever name they call Him. After all, we're all children of one Heavenly Father." In making that assumption, they deprive God of the right to have any say in the matter. Even though Christianity, Hinduism, and the various other religions of the world hold conflicting views of what God is like and what He requires of men, they lack the simple logic to see that, if God exists at all, His truth is one; that He alone has the right to say who He is and what He requires. To deny this is to deny Him the right to be God at all.

But why should Christianity be imposed on

all, to the exclusion of every other approach to God? What the non-Christian religions find intolerable is the intolerance of Christianity in believing that it has the exclusive keys to heaven. Though they may give Jesus more or less honor and respect as a great teacher or even a prophet, they consider certain of His words fanatical and self-exalting. Such declarations as, *"I am the light of the world"* (John 8:12) irritate them. They feel it would have been better, and certainly more modest of Him, to say, "I am one of the spiritual and moral lights of the world." Strangely enough, even some who profess to follow the teachings of Jesus blandly ignore His unequivocal statement, *"I am the way, the truth, and the life: no man cometh unto the Father, but by me"* (John 14:6). Such words are totally unacceptable to non-Christians. And some nominal Christians unthinkingly say that all religions are equally good and lead to God.

Now two laws that are contradictory to each other cannot be equally true and acceptable. We grant this in the physical realm. The law of gravity is singular and exclusive of any contrary law or theory.

If Christ actually is the only way to God, and not one of many ways, then no other claims or ways contrary to His are acceptable. We who are His followers should not weakly concede that He was one of the great men like Buddha, Allah, Ghandi—all of whom were born of earth and still lie in their graves. Jesus Christ was born of heaven and earth, lived a unique life, and rose from the grave. His claim to exclusiveness was not that of a megalomaniac but of God in the flesh. All the rest, whom some foolishly place in the same category as Christ, never made the claims He made for Himself. They couldn't have authenticated them by their works and the resurrection, as Christ did. They knew they had human limitations. But Christ showed not the slightest hesitation in claiming that He was God in the flesh, the light of the world, the only way of salvation.

Christ also claimed that His disciples would be like Him. In Matthew 5:14 He told them, *"Ye are the light of the world."* We who truly believe in and follow Him are the bearers, the conductors, of His own light. We have an exclusive mission, for we are the only hope of the world, as we faithfully proclaim the Gospel. In order for this world's darkness to be dispelled, we must let our light shine before men.

A woman who came to know Christ as her Savior returned home full of joy—that unique gladness that overflows the heart of a repentant sinner. After a few weeks, she expressed a desire to leave the community in which she lived because it was so sinful. When her pastor heard this, he said with some severity, "How would you like it if the city removed all the lights from the dirty and bad streets and left lights only in the good neighborhoods where no crimes are committed? Didn't Christ say, *'Ye are the light of the world'?"* The woman accepted the rebuke, and some time later said to her pastor, "Now there are two lights that shine in our street." She had led a soul to Christ.

The only hope of lighting the darkness of your heart and life is Christ. There is no other light. Christ is the only Savior from sin. He alone can lift that burden from your heart; it was for that purpose that He came into the world. Until you allow Him to come into your life, you will never find true fulfillment. Try the light of Christ. Believe in Him and find real meaning for your life. Then you, too, will become light—perhaps the only light in your neighborhood, your society, your family. Once you begin to live the illumined Christian life, others will see it, and some will be drawn to the Christ whose light shines through you. His claims are exclusive because He is God. Read His Word and let Him speak for Himself. Don't try to tell God that all roads lead to Him. Let Him tell you whether this is so or not. And there is only one place where you can find this out, and that is in the Bible.

WHEN THE STORM HITS

WHEN everything is going well with us, we really don't know what stuff we're made of. It's only in times of stress that our true nature comes out.

Take the Apostle Peter for instance. He had repeatedly and emphatically declared to Christ that he loved Him and would follow Him to the death. But when his protestation of loyalty was put to the test, he failed miserably. It happened after Jesus' arrest, when Peter followed at a distance to see what would happen to Him. As Peter stood outside warming himself at a fire with Jesus' enemies, he denied even knowing Him. It was the same Peter that had made such a fine protestation of love to the death. But at the crucial moment he revealed what he was really made of.

Another occasion when Peter saw himself for what he really was, was in a storm on the Sea of Galilee. At three in the morning Christ's disciples were in danger of drowning, when they saw

Christ walking toward them on the water. Peter, again eager to demonstrate his faith, wanted to walk to Christ on the water. *"Come,"* said Christ. But after a step or two Peter looked at the storm instead of Christ, and began to sink. Christ reached out His hand and brought Peter safely to the boat. I don't think Peter ever forgot His rebuke, *"O thou of little faith, wherefore didst thou doubt?"* (Matthew 14:31). Peter's courage and bravery quailed before the force of the wind and waves. The storm reveals the quality of a man.

I wonder why Christ allowed the tempest, since He was God and could have prevented it. When life's storms hit us, we send up a complaining "Why me, Lord? What have I done, that I should be punished in this way?" It would be better to rephrase the question and ask, "What do you want me to learn from this, Lord?" Is He showing us something we couldn't have learned otherwise?

Peter never said a word in answer to Christ's rebuke. He accepted Christ's judgment of him as a man of little faith. But now that he had been shown his weakness, he could seek to overcome it. How can we correct our faults if we're blind to them? Pain is beneficial because it makes us aware that something is wrong with us. The source of pain is the love of God. When we are afflicted, let's stop and ask God why He allowed it; what He wants us to learn from it. Let's accept it as a blessing and not a curse.

Some of the greatest benefits to mankind

have had their source in men who have experienced great affliction. The German poet Goethe said, "I never experienced affliction that did not turn into a poem." The music that elevates man to heaven has often come from afflicted hearts.

When Dr. Moon was at the height of his useful career he was suddenly stricken with blindness. At first he couldn't understand why God had allowed such a terrible thing to happen to him. But in the darkness he began to think of others who were blind, and to wonder how he could help them. The result was the discovery of an alphabet that is now enabling the blind to read.

He was like that bird that had no interest in learning the song its master wanted to teach it while its cage was full of light. Its master covered the cage to darken it. He then whistled the same song over and over until the bird learned it by heart. When it could repeat it note for note, the owner uncovered the cage and the bird sang it beautifully. This is an illustration of the way God sometimes deals with us. He darkens the cage of our lives in order to teach us some divine song.

A little faith will do for calm weather, but not for the tempest. How easily we're lulled unto thinking our faith is equal to anything, until God allows some crisis in our lives to show us our need of spiritual growth. Under normal circumstances Peter would never have accepted the Lord's verdict that he was a man of little faith. Small faith begins courageously enough, but in a storm it gives way to fear. Little faith is easily puffed up, but a gust of wind deflates it.

But the revelation of your little faith should not discourage you. Christ rebuked Peter for his little faith, but He didn't forsake him. He supported him and brought him safely to the boat. No doubt the rest of the disciples were equally afraid. But Peter was the only one who thought of walking on the water. Why the Lord didn't allow him to succeed was possibly to teach him humility. Perhaps one of the reasons Peter wanted to take this daring step was to achieve a certain distinction. Instead, Christ allowed him to suffer defeat, and called him one of little faith.

God can use even our little faith in a wonderful way if we place it in His strong and omnipotent hands. But our achievements of faith will depend on our motives. If we want to achieve distinction, He will allow us to sink in order to teach us that it is not our faith that can achieve great things for Him, but Christ, who is the object of our faith and supports it in the storms of life. We should be concerned not only about the quantity of our faith but also about its quality. Ask yourself in all honesty, does your faith aim at your own selfish distinction or does it aim at the glory of God? Only then will God honor it.

RIGHT HAND OR LEFT, WHERE WILL YOU STAND?

THE town of Pisa, Italy, is famous, of course, for its leaning tower. Not so well known, but far more significant, is a painting on the wall of a cemetery there. The artist has depicted the last judgment, with Christ, the Virgin Mary, the Twelve Disciples, and a number of angels. Groups of people are coming out of their graves, some going to the right and others to the left of the scene. But there appears to be some confusion. Some who thought they belonged on the right, destined for heaven are being shifted back to the left, destined for hell—and vice versa.

What was the basis for their judgment? For that we have to look in the Bible. Christ said, "*Not every one that saith unto me, Lord, Lord, shall enter into the kingdom of heaven; but he that doeth the will of my Father which is in heaven*" (Matthew 7:21). The Italian artist was inspired by his vivid imagination and the prophetic words of the 25th chapter of Matthew.

The basic teaching is that, at the end of the age, at the last judgment, men will be divided into two classes: those on the right, who will enjoy eternal life with God, and those on the left, who will be thrown into the lake of fire in the company with the devil.

What is the criterion that determines where you will go? In Matthew 25, it is evident that God will not judge you according to your professed knowledge of Him, but according to your genuine faith in Christ as evidenced by your behavior toward your fellow man. Your gifts to charity, your mere philanthropy, are not what will commend you to God, but only that philanthropy that is the direct reflection of your faith in Christ. Faith without works is dead, and words without faith is without merit in God's sight. Scripture nowhere says you can behave like God and believe like a devil, and consider yourself a good person. You can't separate the works of faith from faith, nor faith from its logical outcome of producing good works.

In the day of judgment, Christ will say to those who have confessed a faith in Him that is followed by actions, *"Come."* But to those whose profession of faith has been merely verbal He will say, *"Go."* The hypocrites, those who are Christians in word only, may think their entrance into heaven is secured because they once raised their hand in an evangelistic meeting, or even went so far as to join a church. If that's as far as it went, they were never truly born again, and cannot see the kingdom of God. But those who, from the love of Christ, quietly bound up the wounds of their fellow men, will find to their surprise that Christ regards their deeds of charity as done unto Him.

It's not so important how eloquently you glorify God with your lips, but how you cause others to glorify Him because you practice what you preach. Your prayers are not worth anything unless they produce in you that purity of life that makes others want to pray. The important thing is not the relationship you think you have with God, but the practical expression of God's love that leads others to believe in Him because of your life.

I say "life," and not the sporadic acts of charity you may do to appease God or impress yourself and others. You can't be like that merchant who became rich by defrauding others and then, to quiet his conscience, built a fine church in his village. Nothing you can do can erase your sins of the past. Only by appropriating the work of Christ on the cross can your heart be cleansed from sin. Once you have truly received Him as your Savior, you are regenerated, born again. Whatever good works you do from that moment on are in reality done by Christ who dwells within you. Then your service to your fellow men becomes an ever-flowing fountain. It emanates from Christ Himself and is done for love of God and neighbor.

Martin of Tours was a man in whom faith and works combined to make him a true Christian. One day he met a beggar who asked for alms.

Martin didn't have any money, but he saw that the beggar was freezing, so he gave him what he had. He took off his soldier's overcoat, old and faded as it was, cut it in half, and wrapped half around the beggar. During the night Martin had a dream. He saw heaven opened, and Christ wearing half an overcoat. One of the angels asked, "Lord, why are you wearing that shabby old coat?" And Christ answered, "Because my servant gave it to me." It was only a dream, but it illustrates the truth that Christ taught, that whatever we do for others in His name, He accepts as a gift to Him.

Do you have that genuine faith in Christ that prompts you to show His love in practical ways to those in need? Right hand or left—on which side will you stand in the Day of Judgment?

DO YOU REALLY KNOW WHAT LOVE IS?

TWO brothers were playing together when one suggested they do something their parents had forbidden. Without their knowing it, their father was listening.

You'd better be good," said one, "or Daddy won't love you."

"Jack, come here a minute," called the father. "I heard what you said to your brother, and it isn't true."

"But Dad, if we're bad, will you still love us?"

"Yes, of course. The only difference is that, when you're good I'll love you with a love that makes me happy; and when you're bad I'll love you with a love that makes me sad."

If you love your children only when they're good, you're laying the groundwork in their character for deceit and insecurity. They may try to live up to your standards outwardly, but they'll instinctively hide their wrongdoing from you in order to win your approval. And the fear that any misconduct on their part will result in the loss of your love will undermine the sense of security that is so necessary to a child if he is to grow up with any confidence in his worth as an individual. Never hold the loss of your love over a child's head to make him toe the mark. Even though you must punish him, let him know you do it in love, to correct him, and not as an indication you are rejecting him.

That's how God loves. *"Whom the Lord loveth he chasteneth,"* not in anger, but *"for our profit"* (Hebrews 12:6, 10). He doesn't cease to love us when we sin, but seeks to bring us to repentance and conformity to His will. That's not the way of the world, of course. Most people love those who love them; they love only as long as others live up to their expectations; and when someone offends them, or no longer serves their needs, they stop loving.

True love delights to give, to benefit others; it never exploits. It is saddened when the person loved does something to destroy mutual harmony, but it doesn't cease to love on that account. It seeks for reconciliation rather than taking refuge in hurt pride.

Many couples are held together, not by real love but by self-gratifying love. They seek what the other partner can give in the way of satisfaction and service. And when one ceases to serve the other, the quarrels begin that all too often result in separation. The highest standard of love is to live, not as one who demands to be served, but as one who serves.

This is true in all relationships of the individual, whether to his family, to society, to his country, to the church, or to God. Don't always be looking at people with the attitude of "What can they do for me?" Instead, ask yourself, "What can I do for others?" Only then will your life be happy. And remember that charity begins at home. Don't keep all your congeniality and generosity for your business associates and friends, and be a grouch at home. Don't use your wife as a servant, and your children as outlets for your ill humor. You may protest that you love them, but your actions belie your words. Do something that will make your home the cheerful, encouraging place it ought to be.

Maybe your life is unhappy because you've made it so. What you feel in your heart is what gives worth to life; but if you lack the will to love, and think only of your own selfish gratification, you're never going to be satisfied.

Here's an illustration of love in action. A well-to-do businessman gave a fine car to his brother. One day when he went to the place he'd parked the car, he saw a ragged boy looking the car over with great interest. Instead of saying, "Get away from that car, kid," he smiled at the youngster.

The boy was the first to speak. "Is that car yours, Mister?" "Yes, it is," was the reply. "What did it cost?" was the next question. "Nothing," said the man. The boy looked at him curiously and said, "You don't look like the kind of guy who would steal a car." The owner laughed and said, "No, it was a present from my brother." The boy seemed incredulous. "Do you mean to say he gave it to you as a present, and it didn't cost you anything?" "That's right."

Then the boy said the most surprising thing of all: "I sure do wish I could be such a brother as yours." One might have expected him to say, "How I wish I could have such a brother as yours." The man asked him what he meant, and he explained: "I'll tell you. My youngest brother had polio and he can't walk to see all the shops in town and enjoy the toys, at least by seeing them in the windows. How I wish I had a car like this to take him around. Our father died, and we won't get any presents this Christmas. But at least I can walk along the streets and enjoy the shop windows; my brother can't even do this. That's why I'd like to be to my brother what your brother was to you."

The man's heart was touched. He went to the boy's home and saw to it that they had a good Christmas. He kept up his friendship with them, and thus the older boy's generous spirit was rewarded. Anyone with such an unselfish love can't be unhappy, no matter how poor he may be. Unhappiness is not a matter of lacking material things; it's a psychological matter. Neither the abundance of possessions nor the lack of them determines happiness, but one's attitude toward them.

Had Christ loved only those who loved and served Him, He wouldn't have loved any of us, because men don't love God instinctively and naturally. All that sinful men can do is to respond to God's love. God took the initiative to love us by dying on the cross for us, sinful though we are by nature. When we accept His love by accepting the work He did on the cross, His divine love is born in our hearts. Sinful, selfish, and hypocritical love is replaced by God's love.

Perhaps you think of yourself as a loving person. But if this love has simply originated in you, it is earthy, and in the final analysis will be found to be self-serving. But if it has been implanted by God, it will be a love that first of all satisfies God, then others, and as a result your own self If you will accept God's love by receiving Christ as your Savior, you will begin to learn what love really is.

What shall it Profit

HOW TO GET THE MOST JOY OUT OF LIFE

A STUDENT of Ancient Greek in an English university surprised his teacher by his rapid grasp of the subject. When asked if someone were helping him, he mentioned his uncle. The professor said he'd like to meet him, and a date was set. The teacher was astounded with the uncle's knowledge of Greek. "What work do you do?" he asked.

"I'm an itinerant preacher. I preach God's Word." Dismayed that such a gifted man should waste his time preaching, the professor blurted out, "Man, you're a fool!"

The wise preacher retorted, "In which world, Professor?"

Each one of us belongs primarily to one of two worlds, the eternal or the temporal, the world of the spirit or the world of matter. The fools of one world are often the wise men of the other. One of these worlds has the preeminence in your life. Consider Christ's question: *"For what shall it profit a man, if he shall gain the whole world, and lose his own soul?*" (Mark 8:36) This was not a part of one of Christ's sermons. He had not been speaking of the value of the soul. He was facing another issue when He asked His disciples, "*Whom do men say that I am?*" (Mark 8:27). Peter, understanding the importance of the question, gave the right answer: "*Thou art the Christ*" (Mark 8:29). Jesus praised Peter for his spiritual discernment, saying, "*Blessed art thou, Simon Barjona*" (Matthew 16:17).

But soon after that He began to tell His disciples of His coming death on the cross. Immediately Peter, who had just been blessed for his confession of faith, presumed to judge the Lord. "*Be it far from thee, Lord: this shall not be unto thee*" (Matthew 16:22). It is as though he were saying, "You, the mighty Messiah, would let your enemies murder you on the cursed cross? This is totally unacceptable to me, at least!"

And the same lips that had just addressed a blessing to Peter now spoke in severe judgment: "*Get thee behind me, Satan: thou art an offence unto me: for thou savourest not the things that be of God, but those that be of men*" (Matthew 16:23). Christ continued to tell Peter, as He had been intimating all along, the purpose of His incarnation. "I was born to die. If I avoid death, I cannot fulfill the purpose for which I came into the world." His actual words were, "*The Son of man must suffer many things, and be rejected of the elders and chief priests and scribes, and be slain, and be raised the third day"* (Luke 9:22).

After this conversation with Peter, the Lord defined the first condition of Christian discipleship. *"If any man will come after me, let him deny himself, and take up his cross daily, and follow me"* (Luke 9:23). Someone will always try to dissuade us from doing what we should, from fulfilling the purpose of our life. For Christ the cross was a must; for us it is an option. But with the exercise of our option we must be willing to bear the consequences of our choice.

There are many things a man can achieve without Christ. He can become a successful businessman and grow rich. But in the process his soul can grow lean and hungry. You don't need prayer to become rich. But wealth without prayer can never bring happiness to your soul. Many a rich man without God has died unhappy. There is a poverty even in abundance. When wealthy Croesus lay dying he cried, "O world, you promised that wealth would bring me satisfaction. But now it has become a disappointment."

You can acquire power and fame without Christ. You may even agree with the poet who said that he would prefer to be king in hell than a servant in heaven. But a king in hell will still be reduced to a state of unending misery, while a servant of God in heaven will not be conscious of servitude but only of fulfillment and joy. Money and power bring relative enjoyment on earth, but it is a selfish and short-lived one. It is not true satisfaction.

Christ never condones unethical or dubious methods of acquiring wealth or authority. It's far better to have less, with a clear conscience. Christ is the fulfillment that both rich and poor need. Unfortunately, the poor often recognize this more than the rich.

However, along with Christ comes the cross. For the Christian, the cross means redemption and self-surrender. It is saying to God, "Not my will, but thine be done." And strange as it may seem, this brings the greatest peace and satisfaction of all, for through our self-giving God can begin to do great things in us and through us, for His glory and our joy.

When Christ said, *"For what shall it profit a man, if he shall gain the whole world, and lose his own soul?"* the "if" was purely suppositional. No man can gain the whole world. Christ was indicating that anyone's purpose in seeking satisfaction apart from Him is impossible of realization.

But what does it mean to lose your soul? Exactly the same thing you have in mind when you say, "I've lost my eyes." Your eyes are still there, but you can't see. And when your only care is for the things of this world, your soul still exists, but it has no communion with God. Satan wants neither your money nor your fame. He wants your soul in order to keep it from union with its Creator. He knows that without such union you cannot enjoy either earth or heaven. But with it, God will enable you in the fullest sense to enjoy both.

IDEALISM VS. REALISM

FRANCE is a nation with a threefold ideal: "Liberty, equality, brotherhood." But this aspiration is not the exclusive property of the French; it is the desire of every living person. The idea of slavery is abhorrent to us. We hate the very thought of being looked down upon as a member of an inferior class. To be at ease with our world, we need to feel that those among whom we live are not our overlords or enemies but our friends.

Take that first concept—liberty. Is there any society in which true liberty prevails? And what about equality? Where will you find a community in which there is no snobbery or exclusion on the grounds of race, religion, or possessions? As for human brotherhood, how can we claim to have fulfilled that dream, when in the past 4,000 years or so there have been only 300 years of universal peace? The ideal of liberty, equality, and brotherhood is a utopia, not possible in a world like ours.

However, we need not despair of being able to realize these dreams as individuals. True liberty, genuine equality, and unbroken brotherhood can be found in Christ. Only through Him can we realize these ideals.

Modern man in pursuit of liberty seeks to curtail the authority of the powers that be. He wants his freedoms spelled out in constitutions and laws. He feels that the right of self-determination makes him really free. But the man who has secured the right to vote without being dictated to is not necessarily free. It is possible for him to be a free citizen and yet a moral slave. This is exactly what we experience even in the so-called free nations. We have become free slaves, free to bury ourselves. Freedom of choice can lead to death, if we choose the broad road that leads to destruction.

In order for us to become truly free, the Apostle Paul tells us, we must become slaves. Of whom? Of God. What does he mean by this seemingly paradoxical statement?

In the first place, he says, when we are under the law, it is just like being in prison. We want to do what the law forbids, for that is our nature. I'm speaking of the Old Testament law, of course, given by God to Moses and recorded in the first five books of the Bible. You have only to read the Old Testament to see how God's chosen people broke His laws over and over again. I repeat, that is man's nature.

A cow's nature is to eat grass. You can't make her eat meat. And the nature of the sinner is to sin, and that includes the free citizen who is a slave to his sinful nature. He is free to obey or disobey, but since his nature is sinful he is enslaved in his power of choice, which more often than not yields to the temptation to sin. And if at any time he chooses to resist temptation, it's usually not because he doesn't desire to sin, but because he's afraid of the punishment inflicted by the law. The law is a schoolmaster, a stern disciplinarian.

Is there any way out of this enslavement? In writing to the Galatian Christians Paul assures them that there is. *"Ye are all the children of God in Christ Jesus."* he tells them (Galatians 3:26). You were set free from the law when you became children of God. Your so-called freedom before that was actually a willing slavery to evil. Now your freedom is a slavery to good, to the will of God. How did this come about? By becoming sons of God you have acquired the nature of God. *"Wherefore thou art no more a servant, but a son"* (Galatians 4:7). By becoming a son or daughter of God, you become really free. But how does one become a child of God?

The Bible has the answer to that also: *"By faith in Christ Jesus"* (Galatians 3:26). Faith in who He is—the Son of God, who is God incarnate—and in what He has done for you on the cross in offering Himself as a sacrifice for your sin, sets you free from the law of sin and death. You are born again as a child of God, and then you are truly free to choose the good you were power less to do before. Your inclinations are changed at the very root, because God's Holy Spirit now dwells within you, and you have become a partaker of the divine nature.

Among the children of God there is true equality. God inspired the Apostle Paul to say, *"There is neither Jew nor Greek, there is neither bond nor free, there is neither male nor female: for you are all one in Christ Jesus"* (Galatians 3:28).

Our world is divided into two ideologies with regard to equality. There are those who believe that economic and social equality must be brought about by the state, through force. Others believe that equality is achieved, not by reducing all men to the same level, not by bringing the high down to the level of the very low, but by the high helping the low to improve their level of attainment. The first is the equality of slavery; the second the equality of free action, based on the willingness of both high and low to cooperate.

The state, by confiscating the property of the rich and giving it to the poor, doesn't achieve true equality, because afterward both classes become slaves of the state. Let's not be so quick to divorce realism from idealism. We are in a world full of inequalities of every nature. Among men, not all are equally endowed with intelligence or ability. What would happen if all men had been created equally smart or equally stupid? My guess is that it would produce a state of stasis, in which no progress would be possible, since all men were identical and would see no need for improvement.

We are living in a world of inequality, in which only one equality is possible, equality in Christ. This is the equality of our right as children of God. One child may be smaller, another bigger, but both have the same rights of inheritance from the Father. Every man has the right to become a child of God, whether he be slave or free, Gentile or Jew, white or black. And when we become children of God, in spite of all our physical, acquired, and circumstantial inequalities, we stand on the same basis, that of equality through our common faith in Christ.

Then and only then—when we take Christ as our Savior and, through Him, God as our Father, by faith—do we become true brethren. Brothers are members of the same family, not strangers. When you and I belong to the family of God, all the other blood-bought members of that family are our brothers and sisters in truth.

Be Still and Know That I am GOD

AFRAID TO BE ALONE?

MANY people are, you know. They're afraid of their thoughts, or of the emptiness of their lives. They feel much more comfortable in a crowd. These are the perpetual party-goers, the socializers, the club members who draw their sense of security from being with others like themselves.

Not that it's wrong to socialize. Man is a social creature. Even Scripture affirms that *"it is not good for man to be alone,"* in the sense that he has neither family nor friends (see Genesis 2:18). Christ Himself affirmed the necessity for loving relationships here of believers when he wrote to the churches.

But that is a far different thing from being afraid to be alone. We have to get off by ourselves sometimes to rest, to think, to evaluate our lives. The person who is afraid to do that is not only running away from himself but also from God. Many times the noise of the crowd is too great that we can't hear the voice of God when He wants to speak to us.

A man went inside a telephone booth and dialed the number of a friend. When the connection was made, the friend kept saying, "I can't hear you; speak louder; I can't hear you." All he could hear was the roar of traffic in the background. "Shut the door so I can hear," he said to the caller. In order to hear God's voice speaking to you, you've got to shut the door to the outside world so that its noises won't distract you. If you do this, it could change your whole life. Then when you go back into the crowd, you'll not only be able to listen to what the world has to say, but you'll have something to say to the world that you've personally heard from God.

We live in a world that tends more and more to make us into impersonal beings. We become one number among many. The tendency is to gather into large cities and become allied with those large corporations or associations that tend to enslave the individual as a whole. We relate to the masses and become estranged from ourselves. Let me ask you a pointed question: Do you know yourself? Others may know you to some degree, but do you really know yourself?

If you want to discover why you were put on this earth in the first place, you've got to do some serious thinking. And in order to discover this, you've got to discover God. How can you do this? By allowing Him to speak to you while He has you alone with the Bible, His Word. But you've got to mean business, for unless you're in earnest about it you'll still find yourself alone. *"Ye shall seek me and find me when ye shall search for me with all your heart,"* God promises (Jeremiah 29:13).

So before you take up your newspaper in the morning, let Him speak to you through the Scriptures. Talk to Him before you talk to men. Do this every day, and I promise you, you won't be alone any longer. God will meet with you and set you on the right path for the day. If Jesus felt the need to withdraw from the crowds and commune with His Father, how much more should you and I? However, the newspapers, magazines, radio, and TV, as well as those with whom we associate day by day, all tend to entice us away from spending time alone with God.

Have you ever noticed something odd about even the most respectable newspapers, novels, or magazines—not in what they print, but in what they omit? They urge the most ethical conduct, or set forth heroes and heroines of impeccable virtue, but for the most part they are written as though God didn't exist as a factor to be taken into men's consideration at all. They simply omit all reference to Him, blandly assuming that human values are self-authenticating, and that man is responsible only to society but not to his Maker.

And then there are those publications that disparage the clergy with faint ridicule, as weaklings who lack the courage to take a stand when great issues confront them, but who simply preach pious platitudes and sometimes lead hypocritical lives. Current humor often delights in clever sacrilege, which undermines respect for God and His Church. Christians must be alert to spot these tendencies and not allow themselves to be influenced by them. They often win grudging admiration for their cleverness, but that's where the very danger lies. You can be too much a lover of cleverness, at the expense of your soul.

Saint Augustine often prayed, "Lord, save me from my wicked self." Such self-evaluation can only come to a man as he confronts himself in the mirror God holds up to him when he is alone with Him. Another saint is said to have prayed, "Lord, save me from that good man, myself." He was praying to be delivered from self-righteousness. When we are alone with God and allow Him to speak to us, we realize how imperfect we are. Then, when we are with others, we won't be bragging about ourselves but will give glory to God for the work Christ has performed in our hearts.

A little girl and her father were returning from the funeral of their dearly loved mother and wife. Some kind neighbors invited them to spend a few days with them, so they wouldn't be alone in the house with all its sad memories. However, the father decided it would be better to go home.

That night the father placed the little girl's bed next to his, but neither could fall asleep. Finally the child said, "Daddy, it's dark, I can't see you. But you're there, aren't you?" "Yes, dear, Daddy's here right next to you. Go to sleep." The little one finally dropped off, but after that, in the darkness and the depth of his sorrow, the father in tears said aloud, "O Heavenly Father, it's so dark, and my heart is overflowing with sorrow. But You're there, aren't You?" And immediately there came to him a passage from the prophet Isaiah: *"Fear thou not; for I am with thee: be not dismayed; for I am thy God: I will strengthen thee; yea, I will help thee; I will uphold thee with the right hand of my righteousness"* (Isaiah 41:10). That was God's reassurance to him in the darkest hour of his life. But what if he had never meditated on God's Word, never committed some of its promises to memory, never spent time alone with his Heavenly Father previously? There would have been no word to comfort him in the dark.

You will not hear the voice of God in the midst of the noisy crowd. *"Be still and know that I am God,"* the Psalmist was told (Psalm 46:10). Shut yourself in somewhere until you, too, come to know God through Jesus Christ as your Savior.

IS THERE REALLY A PERSONAL DEVIL?

THE unseen spiritual world is a great mystery. Some people choose to ignore it altogether. But no matter how you try to evade the issue of the origin of evil, outside of you and within you, there comes a time when you're forced to reckon with the powers that motivate your beliefs and actions.

There are two external powers that you've got to face when you're alone with your thoughts. One is God and the other is Satan. Many people profess belief in God, but relatively few believe in the devil. That's precisely why he can operate freely, without opposition from most people.

If you don't believe in the devil as a separate individual or entity, it may be because you've assimilated him into your own nature. As a French priest put it, "If I didn't believe in Satan, then I should have to conclude that I am my own devil." Unfortunately, many people have come into such harmonious agreement with Satan that they no longer have any desire for God.

When God created man, He made him for Himself. And as long as man obeyed God, he would have shared His life, joy, and fellowship. But God didn't want man to be a robot, obeying Him because he had no choice in the matter. He wanted man to be free to choose God's will or to reject it. No one values enforced love and obedience—least of all God. Unfortunately man chose to ally himself with the devil. He believed Satan rather than God, and he has been reaping the tragic consequences ever since. His natural bent is now toward sin; he loves his own way rather than God's way; he has chosen to be a child of the devil, whether he realizes it or not.

When Satan possesses a man's heart, that man seeks the things of earth in preference to the things of eternal value. He embraces a life of sin, whose end is death. By "sin" I do not necessarily mean that he commits murder, theft, or adultery—though a great many do. Sin is simply a turning from God, whether it manifests itself in self-righteousness or flagrant crime. He is like a man wandering through a beautifully landscaped cemetery, willfully ignoring the fact that it is the abode of the dead.

In fact, you can find his counterpart in the demoniac of Gadara, whose story is told in Luke 8:27-39. He lived in the graveyard by choice—a torment to himself and an object of dread to others. One day Jesus passed by that way, and the demoniac called out to Him. It's strange that this man, crazed as he was, understood who Jesus was. He cried, *"What have I to do with thee, Jesus, thou Son of God most high? I beseech thee, torment me not."*

How strange that he could recognize who Jesus was, and yet regard Him as his tormentor rather than his friend and possibly deliverer. Demon-possessed though he was, however, his ability to acknowledge Jesus as the Son of God was a hopeful sign. The Apostle James, you remember, confirmed the fact that even the demons believe in the existence of God. This is the basic ability God continues to give to the sinner in spite of his spiritual deadness. No matter how enslaved you may be to Satan, you have the God-given ability at this very moment to recognize the Christ I am seeking to present to you. Call out to Him as He passes by. No matter how dead you are, you can recognize life. Of course, you may consider the life He offers as torment. That's because darkness is afraid of light. Satan has so blinded man that he looks upon his liberator as his tormentor. Only the ignorant would look upon the doctor who wanted to heal them as a tormentor. The Gospel offers to free you from this spiritual blindness. After your complete take-over by Satan, God comes again in the person of Jesus Christ in order to free you and make you His child again.

Notice that the demoniac didn't ask Christ to free him. It was Christ who took the initiative to do what was needful. He did it because this man recognized Him as God's Son. When you are first confronted by Christ, you will not know all that He can do for you. The revelation of what His person and work can mean in your life will come by degrees. Simply recognize Him as God's Son and tell Him so. Admit that His presence makes Satan's presence in you rebel because he knows that when Christ comes in he will be expelled. Pray: "Act in my life. Let Satan be cast out of my life and free me from his torment."

He'll do it. You'll see. You'll become a new man, a new woman. You'll be freed from sin and from its instigator, Satan. People will wonder at the change in you, just as the people of Gadara wondered at the change in the demoniac. In his case, the demons that possessed him entered into a nearby herd of swine which ran into the sea and drowned. This made the swineherds and other villagers angry, and they asked Christ to go away. Notice their attitude in Luke 8:35: *"Then they went out to see what was done; and came to Jesus, and found the man, out of whom the devils were departed, sitting at the feet of Jesus, clothed, and in his right mind: and they were afraid."*

Also notice that the former demoniac was now sitting at Jesus' feet. He no longer regarded Him as his tormentor, but as his friend and Lord. But he had to be freed from Satan first in order for this to happen. That's exactly what must take place in your life also. You cannot consider Christ your friend, and sit at His feet, unless you allow Him first to do His saving work in your life.

This picture of the liberated demoniac sitting at Jesus' feet is unforgettable. Only he knew the true value of his liberation. He knew what it meant to be under the domination of Satan, and he knew what it meant to be possessed of God. Only one who has been without God, and then comes into the joyous experience of knowing Him as Savior and Lord and Friend, can appreciate the great relief that floods the soul.

Is there a struggle going on in your soul? If you have no desire to sit at Jesus' feet, it means that you sit at Satan's feet. You may call that nonsense, but Satan gleefully counts you as his own.

The place the former demoniac took at Jesus' feet was instinctive. He felt it was the place of security. In fact, he begged Christ to let him go with Him. But that was the one plea Christ did not grant. He told him to go back home and tell what God had done for him. He wanted him to become a missionary. The man may have been saddened that he couldn't remain near Christ. But actually, when is our Lord nearest to us? It's when we introduce Him to others by telling them what He has done in our life, and assuring them He can save them also. Let Christ free you from Satan, sin, and yourself. And once you are liberated, you will feel His continual presence in your life as you witness to others by your words and deeds of His liberating power from sin and its slavery.

GETTING ALONG IN A HOSTILE WORLD

"I LOVE everybody in the whole world," proclaimed a little three-year-old enthusiastically. The grown-ups looked at her in amusement. They knew such innocence wouldn't last long. Sooner or later she would begin to come up against the harsh facts of life and discover that the loving environment of home is not mirrored in the world outside. Her own attitudes, too, would change, as she no longer found herself the center of an adoring circle of relatives and friends.

This is a confusing age in which to grow up. Old norms of conduct have become outmoded in the eyes of many; family life is no longer the close-knit structure that holds people together. The schools no longer reinforce the virtues that the home used to impart. They give lip-service to doing what is right and just, but they give no firm principles by which young people can be guided as to what is right.

All this has happened because man in his independence from God has fallen to the plane of relativity in determining moral principles. Only God and His law are absolute. Because we have forgotten God in society as a whole, we have become a law unto ourselves. We operate on the principle that what is right for us may not be right for someone else, and vice versa. The principles that guide our life—except in the broadest details of what society as a whole condemns, such as murder and theft—are purely subjective.

Even for the Christian, especially for the child growing up in a Christian home, this can be very confusing. Sometimes we're tempted to think the Christian life would be a lot simpler if God had written down explicit instructions of what to do in every detail of our lives. How should we react to our fellow men, Christian or un-Christian? Sometimes lawyers pull down book after book from their shelves when they have to settle some legal detail, in order to find out exactly what the law says.

The law of the Old Testament that God gave to Moses and the Hebrews was something like that. It was very detailed concerning almost every conceivable relationship of man to man. When Christ came to earth, He fulfilled this detailed law of the Old Testament, without going into detail. Instead He minimized the importance of the details, and enunciated certain basic principles to guide His followers. This gave them the freedom of choice in decision and action.

For instance, in the Old Testament God demanded a tithe, ten percent, of a person's income for the Lord's work. Christ taught that the rich who give large amounts may not give as much as the poor who sacrifice out of their poverty. It depends upon the motive of the giver. Instead of saying that you should give a certain definite proportion of your income for the work of God, Christ said, *"Blessed be ye poor: for yours is the kingdom of God. Blessed are ye that hunger now: for ye shall be filled. Blessed are ye that weep now: for ye shall laugh. Blessed are ye, when men shall hate you, and when they shall separate you from their company, and shall reproach you, and cast out your name as evil, for the Son of man's sake"* (Luke 6:20-22).

Now Christ did not mean that there is blessedness in poverty and hunger, in tears, hatred, excommunication, reproach, and slander. These are evils that God detests as much as we do. But the basis of these beatitudes is that phrase at the end of verse 22: *"For the Son of man's sake."* Christ was saying in effect, "For my sake you should be willing to give even more than is required by the Old Testament Law, and even become poor and hungry if necessary to advance the work of God." However, this is a matter of individual leading from the Lord. Christ never said that in serving Him we should reduce ourselves to the condition of those who need our help, for then we could help neither them nor ourselves.

At the close of His Sermon on the Mount,

Christ wanted to give His disciples a basic principle for getting along harmoniously with others as His followers. He didn't try to fit them all into one rigid mold of conduct, but gave them freedom to choose the degree of their adherence to this basic principle. He made this law so broad that it would cover every conceivable individual situation of human relationships. How we apply this law of God in the specific detailed circumstances of our lives proves to what degree we have identified with Christ, and how truly we are His disciples. Christ doesn't assess our character and sincerity by the pious words we address to Him, but by the way we translate our words into deeds in our relationship with others. For example, He does not believe our protestations of love to Him, if we hate our fellow man. We cannot say we want to do His will in our giving, if we cast every petition for help to the needy into the wastebasket.

Christ's basic law for harmonius co-existence with others is found in Luke 6:31: *"As ye would that men should do to you, do ye also to them likewise."* Matthew states it this way: *"All things whatsoever ye would that men should do to you, do ye even to them: for this is the law and the prophets"* (Matthew 7:12). Christ was saying that the whole law of the Old Testament is summed up in this basic principle. It is not a negative law, like some of the Ten Commandments, but a positive rule of action. No wonder it has been called "The Golden Rule" and "The Royal Law of Christ." All Christianity is summed up in this. It doesn't tell us what not to do, but what we should do. And when we do what we ought, we automatically refrain from doing what we ought not. There is no detail of life that doesn't find its answer in this law. You don't need a lot of volumes of moral precepts. Write this law on your heart and you will have the answer to every problem of human relationships.

It is said that the Roman Emperor Severus was so enchanted by this law when he heard it for the first time that he appointed a reader to repeat it aloud every time someone came before him for judgment. He also ordered it to be written in large letters in the most frequented rooms of the palace and in many public buildings. Though an idolater, this Emperor honored Christ as the one who had told them how to live justly, and he was even disposed to include Christ among the gods.

However, in order to apply this law, a person must know himself well enough to understand what is best for himself. Many people want things that are anything but wholesome, right, and just. What they want depends upon what they are. If you are a thief or a confidence man or a gossip, you can't apply this law, because you wouldn't want others to steal from you, or deceive you, or gossip about you. To apply this law, your own life has to be exemplary. The sinful man can't apply it. It is the law of God's Kingdom, and only those who belong to this Kingdom can be ruled by it.

Who belongs to the Kingdom of God? There's a certain looseness in some people's thinking about this matter. But Christ made this clear to a man named Nicodemus who came to see Him secretly one night. *"Except a man be born again, he cannot see the kingdom of God"* (John 3:3). This is diametrically opposed to the saccharin optimism of a Christmas jingle for children that croons, "Santa Claus says we're all God's children; that makes everything right. So let's give thanks to the Lord above, for Santa Claus comes tonight." Raising children on that kind of sickly sentimentality about God is symptomatic of the ignorance of the age about what God has to say about who are His children, and who are not.

Many people are totally unaware of the fact that before they can honestly call themselves Christians they have to experience a new birth that originates from heaven. *"That which is born of the flesh is flesh,"* Christ told Nicodemus, *"and that which is born of the Spirit is spirit. Marvel not that I said unto thee, Ye must be born again"* (John 3:6, 7). Entrance into God's Kingdom is not by virtue of your birth into the physical world, or into a Christian family, or because you're a member of a Christian church. In order to become a member of the Kingdom of God you must personally accept Jesus Christ as your Savior, through faith in Him as the Son of God who died for your sins. For *"as many as received him, to them gave he power to become the sons of God"* (John 1:12).

In the Golden Rule, Christ is not telling you to make yourself, your appetites and your desires, the basis of what you would want to happen to others—unless you yourself have been cleansed and purified by the grace and blood of Christ. When the miracle of the new birth takes place in you, then you will want to give your all, that others may experience the same salvation. You will more and more want to share God's blessings, spiritual and material, with others. Whatever God has done for you, you will want to pass on to others.

The fable of the fox and the wolf aptly illustrates the way of the world that the Christian is to avoid. It seems a fox was peering into a well from which people drew water by lowering an empty bucket at the top, and pulling up the full one that was at the bottom. By accident the fox fell into the empty bucket and found itself at the bottom of the well. It made a lot of noise trying to get out. A wolf, hearing the noise, looked down and said to the fox, "What are you doing, my sister?" "I'm catching fish," was the sly answer; "Come down to help me." "How can I?" asked the wolf. "Jump into that bucket up there and you'll be down here in a moment." The foolish wolf obeyed, and because it was heavier than the fox it went down and the fox came up and started to run away. "Are you leaving me down here?" cried the wolf. But the fox answered laconically, "That's the way of the world, my friend; when one goes up, the other goes down."

All too often that is precisely the way of the world. It's every man for himself, regardless of the consequence to others. In contrast, we who are

Christians must completely renounce such selfish conduct, and accept as our daily standard The Royal Law of Christ: *"As ye would that men should do to you, do ye also to them likewise."*